AN OPS5 PRIMER

AN OPS5 PRIMER

INTRODUCTION to RULE-BASED EXPERT SYSTEMS

PORTER D. SHERMAN
University of Bridgeport

JOHN C. MARTIN
Philips Laboratories

PRENTICE HALL
Englewood Cliffs, New Jersey 07632

Library of Congress Cataloging-in-Publication Data

Sherman, Porter D.
An OPS5 primer : introduction to rule-based expert systems /
Porter D. Sherman, John C. Martin
p. cm.
ISBN 0-13-638586-9
1. OPS5 (Computer program language) 2. Rule-based programming.
3. Expert systems (Computer science) I. Martin, John C.
II. Title.
QA76.73.057S44 1990 89-22914
006.3'3–dc20 CIP

Editorial/production supervision and
interior design: *Kathleen Schiaparelli*
Cover design: *Wanda Lubelska Design*
Cover logo: *Used with the permission of The Connecticut Technology Institute.*
Manufacturing buyer: *Lori Bulwin*

Trademark Information

Sienna OPS5 Compiler is a registered trademark.

Printed in the United States of America
10 9 8 7 6 5 4 3 2 1

ISBN 0-13-638586-9

Prentice-Hall International (UK) Limited, *London*
Prentice-Hall of Australia Pty. Limited, *Sydney*
Prentice-Hall Canada Inc., *Toronto*
Prentice-Hall Hispanoamericana, S.A., *Mexico*
Prentice-Hall of India Private Limited, *New Delhi*
Prentice-Hall of Japan, Inc., *Tokyo*
Simon & Schuster Asia Pte. Ltd., *Singapore*
Editora Prentice-Hall do Brasil, Ltda., *Rio de Janeiro*

CONTENTS

Preface — *ix*

1 Rule-Based Expert Systems — *1*

1.1 Definition of Expert Systems 1
1.2 Examples of Working Expert Systems 3
1.3 Definition of Rule-Based Expert Systems 4
1.4 Knowledge Representation 5
1.5 Storing Information 7
1.6 Defining Rules 7
1.7 The Inference Engine 9
1.8 Working as a System 10
1.9 Advantages and Disadvantages of Rules 14
1.10 Summary 16
1.11 Problems 16

2 Getting Started in OPS5 — *17*

2.1 Working Memory 17

2.1.1 Structure of Working Memory 18
2.1.2 Initialization 19

2.2 Rules 21

2.2.1 Structures of OPS5 Rules 22
2.2.2 Left-Hand Side 26
2.2.3 Introduction to the Rete Matching Algorithm 30
2.2.4 Right-Hand Side 32
2.2.5 Actions Related to Working Memory 33
2.2.6 Actions Related to Input and Output 36

2.3 Summary 38

2.4 Problems 39

3 Intermediate Concepts of OPS5 **40**

3.1 How Rules Control Program Flow 40

3.1.1 The First Rule to Fire 41
3.1.2 Using the LHS to Control Flow 42

3.2 Conflict Resolution 44

3.2.1 Time Tags 45
3.2.2 LEX Conflict Resolution Strategy 47
3.2.3 MEA Conflict Resolution Strategy 48
3.2.4 Choosing a Conflict Resolution Strategy 49
3.2.5 Demons 51

3.3 Arithmetic Operations 52

3.3.1 Using Arithmetic Actions 52
3.3.2 Interaction with WM 53

3.4 Bulk Data Operations 54

3.4.1 File Access 55
3.4.2 Vector Attributes 61

3.5 Summary 65

3.6 Problems 66

4 Programming Techniques **67**

4.1 Iteration and Recursion 67

4.2 Partitioning Rule Sets 71

4.3 Powerful One-Rule Programs 73

4.3.1 Massive Comparisons 73
4.3.2 Traveling Salesman Problem 74
4.3.3 Bubble Sort 77
4.3.4 Population Densities 79

4.4 Summary 81

4.5 Problems 81

5 An Example Program ***82***

5.1 Problem Description 82

5.2 Declaring Working Memory 83

5.3 Adding Some Rules 85

5.4 Summary 98

5.5 Problems 98

6 The Rete Algorithm ***100***

6.1 OPS5 Internals 100

6.2 How the Network is Built 101

6.3 Passing Tokens 105

6.4 Summary 108

7 Advanced Topics ***109***

7.1 Dynamic Rule Building 109

7.2 Simulating Certainty Factors 114

7.3 Interfacing with Other Languages 119

7.4 Interfacing with C 125

7.5 Summary 132

7.6 Problems 132

8 Case Studies ***134***

8.1 Automobile Starting Diagnosis 134

8.2 Grocery Bagging (Synthesis) Program 140

8.3 Real Estate Matching 148

8.4 Summary 161

9 The Next Generation: OPS83 **162**

9.1 Overview 162
9.2 Data Structures 163
9.3 Working Memory 166
9.4 Rules 167
9.5 Control Structures 168
9.6 Functions and Procedures 169
9.7 Using Modules 169
9.8 Customizing Things 171
9.9 Compilation and Linking 171
9.10 External Calls 172
9.11 Summary 174

Appendices **175**

A Using OPS5 on Your System **175**

A.1 Introduction 175
A.2 Using Public Domain OPS5 in a Non-DOS (PC) Environment 175
A.3 Using OPS5 in a DOS (PC) Environment 176

B Debugging an OPS5 Program **179**

C OPS5 Syntax **185**

Index **189**

PREFACE

Artificial Intelligence is a field whose goals seem to move farther away as they are approached. The field has spun off many interesting theories and programming techniques which people are reluctant to call Artificial Intelligence once they see them. One such programming technique is rule-based programming. The paradigm is powerfull, and we feel that it is no more difficult to learn than traditional programming. Because of its simple syntax and data structures, OPS5 is an ideal first language for students learning rule-based programming. Although it has been available primarily in research laboratories for almost a decade, we expect it to be used for years to come.

Our goal in this book is not to teach Artificial Intelligence programming or theories, but to show how rule-based programming can be applied to a variety of problems, with benefits over other programming techniques. Upon mastering OPS5, a student will be prepared to learn more powerful expert systems shells and languages.

Thanks to Dan Neiman and Erik Urdang for their valuable comments on this manuscript. We would like to thank Porter Sherman's expert systems class at the University of Bridgeport as well as the following reviewers for feedback on an earlier version of the manuscript: Glenn D. Bank, Lehigh University and Daniel Niemann, University of Massachusetts. We would like to thank Charles Forgy for two great languages: OPS5 and OPS83. Thanks to the creators of TEX and LATEX, Donald Knuth and Leslie Lamport, which made manuscript preparation a much easier task. Thanks to Child Apte of IBM Watson Research Center and M. Corcoran of the Westchester Campus of Polytechnic University for exposing Porter Sherman to OPS5. We appreciate the assistance of Dan Olson of Electronic Technical Publishing. His LATEX macros for Prentice Hall style made the publishing process much smoother for us. Our editors at Prentice Hall, Valerie

Ashton, Marcia Horton, and Kathleen Schiaparelli, all gave us valuable advice at different stages of writing this book. Thanks to the Computing Resources Group at Philips Laboratories for keeping a great computing environment running smoothly almost every day and night of the year. Finally, we thank our wives, Sally Sherman and Maureen Tracy, for their love and patience through the long process of writing this book.

Porter D. Sherman
John C. Martin

AN OPS5 PRIMER

1

RULE-BASED EXPERT SYSTEMS

1.1 DEFINITION OF EXPERT SYSTEMS

Before one can study a subject, its landscape should be surveyed and reviewed. Let us look at expert systems from this point of view, trying to understand what is really meant by "expert systems" and what they involve.

One place to start is by looking at the name of the subject: *expert systems*. The *expert* part implies intelligence, operative knowledge, and "expertise" in a general sense. *Systems* implies an integrated group of components that are connected to perform together as one. In the case of expert systems, the system is a computer that is controlled by programs; these programs represent the expertise. Therefore, an expert system is a computer system that is programmed to exhibit certain "expertise." In most cases this means solving problems within the framework of the expertise of the system.

This definition is a start toward understanding expert systems, but there are some logistical questions that must be answered before the definition can be accepted. These questions deal with the relationships among the system, the user, and the expert:

1. *What is the operation of the system in relation to the person who will use the system after it is completed?* In most cases, the expert system must be highly interactive with the user and this form of interaction should be simple and not "computer-skill" related. In other words, minimal computer expertise should be required to run the expert system. Not all of the people that these programs will be written for are technically oriented. They will want to have access to a certain "expertise" without having to become computer specialists at the same time. In some cases it may require the use of a separate program as a "front-end" to perform the user interaction. An example of a "front-end" would be a natural language interpreter to act as a translator between the expert system and the user.

The expert system interacts with the user in the solving of a problem in the area of expertise of the system. Usually, this interaction amounts to a dialogue between the user and the expert system, with the result being that the expert system makes a judgment as to a course of action. Another way that an expert system can be used is as a tutor that displays and teaches a certain expertise. The expert system should be given the capability of explaining why it made the judgment that it did and should be able to show how (in a stepwise fashion) it arrived at the conclusion. The complexity of such an explanation system may not be obvious but it can require the equivalent of another expert system on the back end of the main system to provide adequate explanation generation.

2. *What is the relationship between the system and the expert or experts?* Competence in an area is not something that is easily acquired. It is a combination of experience, intelligence, and common sense. Three important reasons for the advent of expert system are directly related to the human nature of expertise. They are:

- The loss of a human expert for reasons such as retirement, promotion, poor health, or resignation means the loss of years of skill and experience.
- It is very difficult for human experts to share their knowledge with more than just a few associates.
- It takes years to cultivate another expert even if it is feasible to do so.

This is why millions of research dollars are being spent annually on expert systems. A whole new subfield of Artificial Intelligence called Knowledge Engineering has evolved to handle the difficult task of extracting knowledge from experts and encapsulating that knowledge in an expert system.

The expert system must allow for modular representation of knowledge to facilitate rapid development. The ideal situation would allow knowledge to be added to or removed from the expert system with minimal disruption of the system's operation. (The term that is commonly used by computer programmers to describe this type of disruption is "side effects." The side effects are unwanted actions that occur when a piece of code is added to or removed from a program that is working correctly. Side effects range from minor formatting problems to major system crashes.) A measure of a good expert system design tool is the ease with which it allows the designer to update the knowledge.

3. *What is the relationship of the expert system to its domain and control environment?* "Domain" refers to the area of knowledge that the expert system deals with. A characteristic of expert systems is that they are tied to a domain: they will fail to arrive at a solution for any task outside their domain. There are two main strategies used in expert system control: forward and backward chaining. The forward chaining strategy will start with a fact (or set of facts) and try to establish a conclusion by relating these facts to the expertise of the system. As an example, consider a system that would determine if a person qualifies for a mortgage when yearly income and yearly debt is known. The system would take the income and debt facts, and match them to a set of qualifiers that are contained within the domain of the system. The system would move forward trying to determine if the mortgage (the goal) could be granted. This illustrates how forward chaining works: start with basic facts and try to arrive at a composite of the facts (goal). In contrast, the backward chaining strategy starts with the composite of facts (goal) and works backward through the domain trying to verify the goal. For example, if a mortgage were available, an expert system could search its domain for the people whose facts (income and debt) match the composites (requirements) of the goal. If a piece of information were missing, it would prompt the user for it. Thus the backward chaining strategy starts with a goal and tries to associate the correct facts to that goal.

The designer has the ability to customize or change the control strategy, but usually the choice of an expert system design language is related to the specific control strategy required. In other words, the tool should be selected to fit the problem. It is the expert system designer's responsibility to encapsulate the expert's knowledge within the expert system design language, thus creating an expert system that solves problems within a specified domain.

1.2 EXAMPLES OF WORKING EXPERT SYSTEMS

Expert systems have been around for more than a decade but they have only recently been taken out of the research lab and commercialized. It is relatively easy to design an expert system in an unconstrained environment such as a university or research lab where failure is not disastrous, but in a commercial application, a company or patient's future may depend on the correct decisions obtained from an expert system. Therefore, expert systems have been slowly and cautiously introduced into areas such as business and medicine. In fact, "tools" are the main expert system products offered, while the actual system design is still left to the purchaser of the tools. The following rule-based expert systems are described because they represent working commercial systems.

1. R1/XCON. This was a joint venture by Carnegie-Mellon University and Digital Equipment Corporation; therefore, it was developed in the research lab with the intention of producing a "commercial" product for in-house use at Digital. XCON is used to configure minicomputer systems for Digital. The customer's requirements for a computer system are given to XCON and then the expert system configures a VAX computer. The expert system is composed of three types of rules: operator rules, sequencing rules, and information gathering rules. The accuracy of XCON is quite good, but a group of technical experts still must review the results before a final configuration is accepted.

The power and advantage of XCON is that it embodies expertise that will not be lost because of personnel changes such as promotions. The rule-based structure of XCON allows it to be updated when facts about the VAX product line change. The system enabled Digital to reduce its configuration staff because XCON produces all the paperwork for the configuration, including diagrams and drawings. Also, the staff can work more efficiently since they are now "trouble-shooters" and are released from the redundant, mundane task of being "paper shufflers." XCON is currently written in OPS5. It has thousands of rules and is still growing. The success of XCON has demonstrated that rule-based expert systems are viable approaches to industrial problems.

2. DELTA. This is a rule-based expert system developed by General Electric to help in the diagnosis and repair of diesel locomotives. The system is diagnostic in that it helps the repair technician isolate problems by interacting with an expert system. The system is tutorial in that once the problem is located, it will describe a step-by-step procedure for fixing the problem (it incorporates videodiscs to help with the instruction).

This rule-based expert system has taken the knowledge of a locomotive expert who has spent 40 years in the field and encapsulated it into a program that the mid-level locomotive mechanic can access. DELTA can diagnose more then 80% of the problems that a locomotive will experience and will associate a "degree of certainty" with the diagnosis. This allows the mechanic to view several diagnoses and choose the correct one. Thus it has reduced the downtime that had previously been associated with a locomotive breakdown because now the mechanics do not have to wait for a bona fide expert to become available. It also serves as a training system for new mechanics and as a supplement for semi-skilled mechanics (bringing them up to speed in the shortest time possible). DELTA was developed in LISP and ported to FORTH (an efficient, stack-oriented programming language). It has approximately 1200 rules.

These are just two examples of successful rule-based expert systems that are being used in the commercial world. The applications of expert systems are varied, and as programmers become more skilled in OPS5 program design they will find that there are many domains where rule-based expert systems can be applied.

1.3 DEFINITION OF RULE-BASED EXPERT SYSTEMS

The most common expert system paradigm to date is the rule-based expert system and OPS5 is one of the most popular rule-based expert system design languages. In this section we explain how a rule-based expert system actually works. The concept of rule-based knowledge representation is introduced later in this chapter. The example that will be used is simple and is designed only to give an introductory flavor at this point of the book. A more complicated version that is implemented in OPS5 will be introduced in the following chapters.

There are three main components of rule-based expert systems. They are *facts*, *rules*, and *control*. The *facts* represent the stored knowledge about a problem domain. These facts can be acquired as the expert system is being designed, and they can also be stored as they are accumulated during the running of the expert system program. An example of how facts might be stored in a rule-based system is shown here:

Example 1.1. An example record

```
(Applicant Name- John Smith Address- 25 Lovers Lane SS#- 04742997
  Income- $60,000 Savings- $50,000 Debt- $15,000)
```

```
(Applicant Name- Tom Tucker Address- 5 Colony Road SS#- empty
  Income- $40,000 Savings- $25,000 Debt- $100,000)
```

Rules represent the way the facts are associated with one another, and rules have the ability to create and alter the facts in ways prescribed by the designer. Example 1.2 shows the basic components of a rule that will operate on the facts of type `applicant` in Example 1.1, in the context of a loan expert system. The rule is in an `IF-THEN` form. The rule asks the question: Is the sum of *one-half the applicant's income plus the applicant's savings* 50% larger than the applicant's outstanding debt? If the answer is yes, then the action that is described in the THEN section is taken: The applicant's name will be placed on a tentative approval list and the applicant's status is changed from pending to tentative. If the answer is no, then the rest of the IF-THEN rule is ignored and no action is taken.

Example 1.2. An example rule

```
 [IF pattern #1 (applicant's (income/2 + savings) is
                50% GREATER THAN  (applicant's debt))
THEN action #1  (put applicant's name on Tentative Loan Action List)
     action #2  (change applicant's loan status to tentative) ]
```

There can be many rules in a system and the integrated behavior of these rules (patterns that they match and actions that may take place) is the way an "expert" decision is reached.

The *control strategy* of a system is the form of inference chain (forward or backward) that links the prescribed association of facts (rules). The controlling mechanism exhaustively accesses all the stored facts and rules until no more associations are possible. When there are no more associations, this marks the end of the session with the expert system. The value of the output generated by an expert system is directly related to the accuracy of the stored facts, the breadth of the facts in relation to the domain, and the correctness and completeness of the rules in the system.

The control strategy can begin from facts and build to a conclusion (which is called forward chaining or data-driven control), or the strategy can identify a possible conclusion (or hypothesis) and search through the facts to see if that conclusion is supported (which is called backward chaining or goal-driven control). The choice of strategies is governed by the type of problem and expertise that the expert system is working with.

In the sections to follow, an example of a rule-based expert system will be developed. The example will illustrate how an expert system could be used to advise an organization such as a bank whether a loan applicant is qualified for a loan.

1.4 KNOWLEDGE REPRESENTATION

Extracting knowledge from an expert is a long, demanding task that can require excellent listening and interviewing skills on the part of the knowledge engineer. There may be a tremendous number of hurdles that must be overcome before an expert will feel comfortable enough (consciously or unconsciously) to divulge the "secrets" of his or her "expertise." Examples of the hurdles that occur when extracting knowledge range from distrust of computers, to loss of job security, to selfish protectionism, which is why the psychological view is needed. The complex topic of knowledge extraction is beyond the scope of this book. We will assume for the purposes of this book that a cooperative expert is readily available. For the most part, the programs in this book have used the "expertise" of the programmer who has written the program. This works well for learning and actually helps the designer answer the crucial question: "What is the exact process that the expert uses when solving this problem?" It is often much simpler to solve a problem than to explain how it was solved or why decisions were made when they were made.

Given the assumption that one has the knowledge readily available, we are left with the question of how to represent the knowledge. This question and the discussion that follows deal with one of the criteria that should be used when choosing an expert system design language.

The OPS5 language requires the expert system programmer to store facts in an area of memory called *working memory* (WM). The structure of these stored facts is closely related to a record structure in a database management system. Working memory uses a class and attributes type of record where a class is defined to have a certain number of attributes. The attributes contain the values that represent the facts in the domain. Example 1.3 represents a record of a loan applicant. The category is `Applicant` and there is a list of attributes (related information) for each applicant. Each attribute has an associated value, e.g., the value of the attribute `name` is `John Smith`. Note that the category `Applicant- Name, SS#, Income, Savings, Debt` is cloned for every new instance of the category, and that there is no limit to the number of times a category may be used.

This use of a WM area separate from the control operation of the program allows for convenient maintenance of the system as it dynamically changes, i.e., updating the WM with current facts. But this simplicity also creates problems by representing the facts as records that give knowledge a flat (one-dimensional) appearance. This increases the complexity of system design because the overall associations throughout the domain are hidden from the user and designer: it is difficult to relate the classes, attributes, and facts in WM to specific knowledge concepts.

Example 1.3. Loan applicant record structure

```
(Applicant Name- John Smith Address- 25 Lovers Lane SS#- 04742997
   Income- $60,000 Savings- $50,000 Debt- $15,000 Loan Status- pending)

(Applicant Name- Tom Tucker Address- 5 Colony Road SS#- empty
  Income- $40,000 Savings- $25,000 Debt- $100,000 Loan Status- pending)
```

The preceding two sections have introduced the concepts of "expert system." The main benefit of an expert system is to use the computer to:

- Represent human expertise so that it will never be lost
- Make this expertise available to anybody who has access to the expert system
- Allow the expertise to be maintained as it grows in scope

1.5 STORING INFORMATION

The scenario for storing facts in a rule-based expert system can be likened to developing a record structure in a traditional programming language or database. Essentially you can define an element type with zero or more attributes associated with it. There can be many elements and attributes stored in the memory of the expert system. For example, if the designer wanted to add more credit to the structure used in Example 1.1, it could easily be fitted in as a new attribute to the `Applicant` category:

```
(Applicant Name- John Smith Address- 25 Lovers Lane SS#- 04742997
   Income- $60,000 Savings- $50,000 Debt- $15,000 Loan Status- pending)

(Applicant Name- Tom Tucker Address- 5 Colony Road SS#- empty
   Income- $40,000 Savings- $25,000 Debt- $100,000 Loan Status- pending)
```

Note that `Applicant` defines a unique class and is distinct from other classes that might be added in the future, such as creditors, brokers, loan approval lists, and so on, just as in a regular database. Also, the class `Applicant` can be further specified by name, social security number, street, and so forth. For each name we have a list of attributes that are related to credit information. This data represents the basic facts that are needed about a person so that a loan evaluation can be performed. The values of the attributes may be complete or partial at the start of the running of the system. If the facts are incomplete, then it is up to the expert system to request that the user enter the information that is needed. The values of the facts can be initially stored when the program is designed or they can be dynamically stored as the program runs.

1.6 DEFINING RULES

As already shown, the rules of a rule-based expert system take the form of IF-THEN statements. The IF section looks for associations between certain attributes of the elements stored in memory. Essentially, the IF section invokes a matching process that searches the entire fact memory. The IF section of the rule looks at the facts in memory without affecting what is stored; in other words, the matching of the IF section of the rule will never cause side effects such as altering memory or writing output. Three rules are presented in Example 1.4. Note that in `Rule2`, the `AND` statement is implicit. No matter how many patterns are made in the IF section of a rule, they all have to be true before the THEN section can be processed.

Example 1.4. Three rules

```
Rule1:[IF pattern #1 (applicant's SS# is empty)
     THEN action #1 (query user for applicant's SS#)
          action #2 (store applicant's SS#)      ]

Rule2:[IF pattern #1 (applicant's income is LESS THAN applicant's debt)
          pattern #2 (applicant's savings is LESS THAN applicant's debt)
     THEN action #1  (change applicant's loan status to  "disapproved")
          action #2  (put (applicant's name) on "disapproved"
                     Loan Action List)  ]

Rule3:[IF pattern #1 (applicant's (income/2 + savings) is
                     50% GREATER THAN  (applicant's debt))
     THEN action #1 (put (applicant's name) on "tentative" Loan Action List)
          action #2 (change (applicant's loan status) to tentative)]
```

Note that the number and the order of the patterns in a rule is unrelated to the number of the actions in that rule. Generally speaking, when the IF section of a rule matches with facts in memory, then all of the THEN parts of the rule are processed. One type of THEN action can change the values of facts stored in memory. In Example 1.5, `Rule2` will search the fact memory, finding each instance of a loan applicant. On finding an applicant, the rule will then get the applicant's income and compare it to the applicant's debt. If the comparison shows that the income is greater than the debt, then the rule does not investigate the applicant any further. But if the applicant's income is less than the applicant's debt, then the rule will check to see if the applicant's savings are enough to cover the debt.

Example 1.5. Rule for disapproval of applicants

```
Rule2: [ IF pattern #1 (applicant's income is LESS THAN applicant's debt)
        AND pattern #2 (applicant's savings is LESS THAN applicant's debt)
       THEN action #1 (change applicant's loan status to  "disapproved")
            action #2 (put (applicant's name) on "disapproved"
                       Loan Action List)]
```

When the IF part of this rule finds that both the applicant's income and the applicant's savings are less then the applicant's debt, then the rule will cause a change to the stored facts: the applicant's loan status is changed to `disapproved` and the applicant's name will be placed on the Loan Action List under the subheading `disapproved`. When a rule matches and its actions are taken, the rule is said to have *fired*.

By carefully wording the IF section, the designer of a rule-based expert system can create any structure for the facts in memory, and by choosing the appropriate action to take place in the THEN section of the rule, the designer can achieve any result from any association. The IF-THEN structure of rules is very powerful as well as simple to understand.

1.7 THE INFERENCE ENGINE

So far we have started to build the framework of a loan qualification expert system in relation to the domain: a record structure of the applicant's credit history. We have developed rules to assert specific relationships about the loan applicant's credit history, and depending on the truth of these patterns, action is taken to move the applicant toward or away from loan qualification. Now we must develop a controlling strategy that will establish a systematic interaction between these facts and rules. This controlling mechanism of the rule-based expert system is called the *inference engine* because it follows an inference chain established by the IF patterns of the rules. It carries out three tasks:

- Searching the stored facts and matching the IF patterns of rules to these facts.
- Selection of a single rule that will fire. This is needed because there might be many rules whose patterns match the stored facts but only one rule can be fired during each inference engine cycle.
- Execution of the THEN actions of the selected rule.

The code for the inference engine is not normally modifiable by the expert system designer and the operation of the inference engine is one of the main criteria for expert system design language selection. The facts and rules are created by the designer, while the inference engine is considered part of the compiler or interpreter for the language.

The operation of the inference engine is cyclic. During each cycle it tries to match (associate) the IF patterns of all the rules to the existing facts in memory. When all the matched rules are identified, one is selected to fire. After that rule fires, the inference engine starts another cycle. The inference engine will continue to cycle until there are no more rules that have their IF patterns matched. The expert system will stop when this occurs because it is finished with its analysis of the problem. At this point, the system may or may not have solved the problem. Two key points about this process that the designer should be aware of are:

1. The right-hand side (RHS) of a rule has the ability to change memory. This is important in relation to the inference engine because each cycle operates in exactly the same way: trying to match all the patterns of every rule in the system. An infinite loop can occur if the designer is not careful about his or her choice of the right-hand side of the rule. In general, an infinite loop is a programming error, though infinite loops could be desirable in some applications (in these cases, the computer must be interrupted or reset so that normal control can resume.) The following is an example of a rule that will loop continuously:

```
 [IF pattern #1 (applicant's loan status is disapproved)
THEN action #1 (change applicant's loan status to "disapproved") ]
```

The rule will always fire because the working memory elements will always be updated by the THEN action of the rule. The error in the logic of this example is obvious, but in complex expert systems such errors can be much more subtle. In Chapter 4 we explain in depth how an infinite loop might occur in OPS5.

2. When more than one rule matches, the inference engine must choose a single rule from a group of matched rules. This is called *conflict resolution* and the group of rules that have matched are called the *conflict set*. There are many different ways to approach this problem and the methods available could be an important criterion for expert system language selection. Here are some different approaches that could be used in conflict resolution (although none of them will work in all cases):

- One way to resolve the conflict between rules would be to keep a list of all rules that have previously fired, and have the inference engine exclude from the conflict set any rule that has previously fired. The reasoning behind this is that once a rule acts on the facts, then it would only be redundant for it to fire again and again.
- The *access tags* of the facts could be taken into account. The term "access tag" means that every time a fact is changed, a record of the access time is maintained (it is tagged). The rule whose patterns match the most recently updated facts (last class accessed) will be the one to fire. The reasoning here is in the assumption that the most recently accessed data is the more important data; it is the data that is vital to the present flow of operation and this data must be used immediately.
- Another approach is to look at the order (sequence) of the rules that are stored in the conflict set and select the "earliest" rule that is present, i.e., the first rule on the list. The reasoning here is that the order in which the rules are listed in the source code plays an important role in the way the expert system solves a problem.
- A simplistic approach might be to choose a single rule from the conflict set by random selection.

In different rule-based systems, a combination of all these approaches is used for rule selection. The problems of conflict resolution must be understood by the designer if the full power of the rule-based language is to be used. We will have examples later in this book where different conflict resolution strategies alter the behavior of a program.

1.8 WORKING AS A SYSTEM

A system is the integration of separate parts, all working together for some common purpose. The parts of an expert system that have been defined so far are:

1. The stored facts
2. The rules
3. The inference engine

These are the components of a rule-based expert system and when put together, they represent a working system. Example 1.6 shows the initial facts of Example 1.1.

Note that all the attributes of this Loan Action List are empty since we are in the initial implementation of this system. Also note that each working memory element has been given an access tag so that the inference engine will know which one was updated most recently. (The values of the access tags have been made up for this example.) They signify that the `Applicant` working memory element with the name *John Smith* is the least recently accessed data, while the `Loan Action List` working memory element has been the most recently accessed data; i.e., the larger the access tag value, the more recent the cycle that modified that data.

Example 1.6. Initial facts

```
(Applicant [access tag = 1] Name- John Smith SS#- 04742997
    Income- $60,000 Savings- $50,000 Debt- $15,000)

(Applicant [access tag = 2] Name- Tom Tucker SS#- empty
    Income- $40,000 Savings- $25,000 Debt- $100,000)

(Loan Action List [access tag = 3] Approved- empty
    Tentative Approval- empty Disapproved- empty)
```

The working memory knowledge above can be paraphrased in this way: The class `Applicant` contains two people who are applying for loans. The first applicant is John Smith, who earns $60,000 a year, has saved $50,000, and has an overall debt of $15,000. The second applicant is Tom Tucker, and his credit information follows the same form as John Smith. A list structure that contains approval information is also stored in the memory of this system and it does not contain any information at this moment. Example 1.7 shows the rules that were previously developed for this system.

Example 1.7. Example rules

```
Rule1:[IF pattern #1 (applicant's SS# is empty)
     THEN action  #1 (query user for applicant's SS#)
          action  #2 (store applicant's SS#)   ]

Rule2:[IF pattern #1 (applicant's income is LESS THAN applicant's debt)
      AND pattern #2 (applicant's savings is LESS THAN applicant's debt)
     THEN action  #1 (change applicant's loan status to  "disapproved")
          action  #2 (put (applicant's name) on "disapproved"
                      Loan Action List)]

Rule3:[IF pattern #1 (applicant's (income/2 + savings) is
                     50% GREATER THAN  (applicant's debt))
     THEN action #1 (put (applicant's name) on "tentative" Loan Action List)
          action #2 (change (applicant's loan status) to tentative) ]
```

We will use an inference engine that incorporates all the conflict resolution schemes that were described previously. The inference engine will work in cycles and try to match as many rules as it can during each cycle. When no more matches can be made, the program stops. In the following descriptions, each cycle will be identified, the status of the rules will be explained, and the action that the inference engine will take is described. The symbol • in front of a rule will signify that the rule's patterns have matched in the cycle and the rule is ready to fire. The symbol ○ will signify that the rule's patterns have not matched and the rule will be ignored. Now let us follow the flow of the forward chaining inference engine as it associates the facts with the IF section of the rules:

> First Cycle. The inference engine tries to match all the IF patterns of the rules with current facts that are stored in memory.
>
> • Rule1. Pattern 1 is matched with Tom Tucker because his SS number was not recorded.
> • Rule2. Both patterns are matched with Tom Tucker because Tucker's income is less than his debt and his savings are less than his debt.
> • Rule3. Pattern 1 is matched for John Smith because 1/2 of his income is $30,000 and when added to his savings it gives a total of $80,000, which is greater than 1/2 his outstanding debt ($7500).

The inference engine must decide which rule to fire: `Rule1`, `Rule2`, or `Rule3`. The list of previously fired rules is empty because this is the first inference cycle. Thus, there are no previously fired rules to eliminate during conflict resolution. If we look at the sequence of the rules (first rule in the rule order), then `Rule1` is our choice. Note that the access tags are in sequential order at this point because we assume that they have been loaded this way. Now `Rule1` is selected to fire. This will ask for Tom Tucker's social security number and store the input number as the value of Tucker's `SS#`. This will cause the value of the access tag for `Applicant` Tom Tucker to change to `4` because it was just modified by `Rule1`:

```
(Applicant [access tag = 1] Name- John Smith SS#- 04742997 Income-
     $60,000 Savings- $50,000 Debt- $15,000)

(Applicant [access tag = 4] Name- Tom Tucker SS#- 31103488 Income-
     $40,000 Savings- $25,000 Debt- $100,000)

(Loan Action List [access tag = 3] Approved- empty list Tentative
     Approval- empty list Disapproved- empty list)
```

The inference engine now cycles through the facts and rules again:

> Second Cycle. The inference engine tries to match all the IF patterns of the rules with current facts that are stored in memory.
>
> ○ Rule1. Pattern 1 cannot be matched with any fact (i.e., all the applicants now have SS numbers).
> • Rule2. Both patterns are matched with Tom Tucker because Tucker's income is less than his debt and his savings are less than his debt.
> • Rule3. Pattern 1 is matched for John Smith because 1/2 of his income is $30,000 and when added to his savings it gives a total of $80,000, which is greater than 1/2 his outstanding debt ($7500).

Now the inference engine must decide which rule to fire: `Rule2` or `Rule3`. Only `Rule1` is on the previously fired rules list and it is not in the set of rules to be fired because `Rule1`'s patterns have not matched. The access tags are now compared. The access tag associated with the applicant Tom Tucker is more recent than the access tag associated with applicant John Smith. This causes the inference engine to select `Rule2` (the rule whose patterns match Tom Tucker) to be fired. Note that the action of this rule will change applicant Tucker's status and will update the Loan Approval List, as seen here in Example 1.8.

Example 1.8. Fact memory after the second cycle

```
(Applicant [access tag = 1] Name- John Smith SS#- 04742997
      Income- $60,000 Savings- $50,000 Debt- $15,000)

(Applicant [access tag = 5] Name- Tom Tucker SS#- 31103488
     Income- $40,000 Savings- $25,000 Debt- $100,000)

(Loan Action List [access tag = 6] Approved- empty
      Tentative Approval- empty Disapproved- Tom Tucker)
```

The inference engine now cycles through the facts and rules again:

Third Cycle. The inference engine tries to match all the IF patterns of the rules with current facts that are stored in memory.

- ○ Rule1. Pattern 1 cannot be matched with any fact (i.e., all the applicants now have SS numbers).
- • Rule2. Both patterns are matched with Tom Tucker because Tucker's income is less than his debt and his savings are less than his debt.
- • Rule3. Pattern 1 is matched for John Smith because 1/2 of his income is $30,000 and when added to his savings it gives a total of $80,000, which is greater than 1/2 his outstanding debt ($7500).

Now the inference engine must decide which rule to fire: `Rule2` or `Rule3`. `Rule2` can be eliminated because it is on the previously fired rule list (remember that every rule that gets fired is automatically put on this list by the inference engine and it now contains `Rule1` and `Rule2`). Therefore the only rule left in the conflict resolution set is `Rule3`. The inference engine fires `Rule3` and the status of John Smith is changed to tentative approval. Example 1.9 shows that the loan action list is also updated so that the attribute `approved` now has John Smith's name.

Example 1.9. Fact memory after third cycle

```
(Applicant [access tag = 1] Name- John Smith SS#- 04742997
      Income- $60,000 Savings- $50,000 Debt- $15,000)

(Applicant [access tag = 5] Name- Tom Tucker SS#- 31103488
      Income- $40,000 Savings- $25,000 Debt- $100,000)
```

```
(Loan Action List [access tag = 6] Approved- empty list
      Tentative Approval- John Smith Disapproved- Tom Tucker)
```

The inference engine now cycles through the facts and rules again:

Fourth Cycle. The inference engine tries to match all the IF patterns of the rules with current facts that are stored in memory.

- ○ Rule1. Pattern 1 cannot be matched with any fact (i.e., all the applicants now have SS numbers).
- • Rule2. Both patterns are matched with Tom Tucker because Tucker's income is less than his debt and his savings are less than his debt.
- • Rule3. Pattern 1 is matched for John Smith because 1/2 of his income is $30,000 and when added to his savings it gives a total of $80,000, which is greater than 1/2 his outstanding debt ($7500).

Now the inference engine must decide which rule to fire: `Rule2` or `Rule3`. But all rules are eliminated because they have been fired before. Thus, with no more rules left, the inference engine stops cycling. The problem is solved at this point in relation to the present facts: applicant Tom Tucker has been disapproved while John Smith has been tentatively approved. If the facts were updated, then the inference engine could be started again with a new conflict set and an empty "fired list," and another expert system scenario would begin.

1.9 ADVANTAGES AND DISADVANTAGES OF RULES

The scenario in the preceding section represents a simple example of a rule-based expert system. In this book, we will take a similar, but more complex example and develop it using a specific rule-based programming language: the OPS5 programming language. This extended example will show how the three main components of an OPS5 expert system (*knowledge representation* in terms of facts, *expertise* in the form of rules, and *control* in the form of an inference engine) will integrate into a working system. But first we should look at the advantages and disadvantages of using a rule-based expert system.

Advantages.

1. The domain knowledge and the control mechanism are separated from each other. Domain knowledge refers to the subject that the expert deals with. The control mechanism is the inference engine. An experienced programmer might look at the example in the preceding section and quite correctly state that any high-level programming language could be used to implement the same scenario. The advantage of a rule-based expert system design language is that it allows the designer to change the facts and rules without affecting the control mechanism of the program.

2. It is a non-complex design environment. The IF-THEN rule structure is simple to understand and use. Many problems can be represented in this fashion, some more naturally than others. Also, the storing of facts in memory is a straightforward operation.

3. The control mechanism is embedded and implicit, and it does not require the user to write the inference engine. Rule-based design presents a general shell that allows efficient expert system design compared to other languages. Once the designer becomes proficient in the use of the shell, this proficiency can be transferred (via the shell) to any new problem without having to reinvent the wheel every time. In other words, if a procedural programming language were used, the data structure and control mechanism might have to be redeveloped for each new problem.

With rule-based expert system design, the process for developing rules and following the flow of inferences becomes more obvious with experience. Debugging is the stepwise process of monitoring the rule firings. The designer can verify that the logic of the expert system is being followed by noting the order in which the rules are being fired as well as the values of the access tags of the facts as they are displayed during the inference engine cycles. This can all be done in the interpretive mode for ease of debugging.

Disadvantages.

1. Rules are usually uni-directional. The cycles are performed in a sequential fashion. Though the rule-based expert system can implement both forward and backward chaining, usually it is designed to do one or the other.

2. Computational expense of pattern matching and conflict resolution. The overhead of using OPS5 can cause slower performance than a similar application implemented in C or Pascal. In computer languages, one often trades off speed for power and elegance.

3. Knowledge can be hidden. The representation of knowledge as facts and rules is natural for some types of knowledge, and awkward for others. The relationships among the facts, rules, and the problem to be solved are not necessarily apparent in the structure of a rule-based expert system. Rule-based expert systems must be well documented to allow maintenance and expansion.

4. Large systems rapidly become complex. The clarity of a rule-based system can decrease dramatically as the rules become more complex. As the system gets more rules, control problems increase. Also, system performance usually deteriorates as the number of facts and rules are increased, although not as quickly as one would expect.

1.10 SUMMARY

We have learned that a rule-based expert system is composed of *stored facts*, *rules*, and an *inference engine*. Rule-based expert systems are good at solving problems where there are no obvious algorithms or formulas for solving the problem. If the problem is repetitive and algorithmic, then a general-purpose programming language should be used, not a rule-based expert system. Nevertheless, a problem to be solved by an expert system must be a problem that a human being is capable of solving. Rule-based programming is a programming style, not a magic trick to solve previously unsolvable problems.

1.11 PROBLEMS

1. Given the three reasons for expert systems listed in this chapter, can you think of three more?
2. XCON and DELTA are two examples of successful expert systems. See if you can find examples of at least two more working systems. Include a description of the problem that they solve, and their operation.
3. Explain why the IF-THEN form is often a natural way to express expertise in a system.
4. Why is it important to maintain a record of when a memory element is accessed?
5. Describe how memory, rules, and control work together as a system. How do these three components of a rule-based system interact?
6. How does a cycle relate to the operation of system that you described in problem 5?
7. A disadvantage of using a rule-based system is that "knowledge can be hidden." Explain what this means.

2

GETTING STARTED in OPS5

A *production system* is a variety of rule-based programming as described in Chapter 1. The OPS5 production system was developed at Carnegie-Mellon University (CMU) in the late 1970s by Dr. Charles Forgy. OPS5 stands for Official Production System version 5. There were many production systems in use at CMU, so the word "Official" was meant to be tongue in cheek. OPS5 and its ancestors have been used in many expert systems. At present, there are versions of OPS5 for many machines, including VAX minicomputers, many workstations, IBM-compatible personal computers, and Apple Macintoshes.

Like the rule-based languages discussed in Chapter 1, OPS5 has three main components that the designer must be familiar with. They are the *working memory*, the *rules*, and the *inference engine*. In the following sections we discuss these components in relation to the example developed in Chapter 1.

2.1 WORKING MEMORY

In previous discussions of rule-based languages, the program memory was referred to as fact memory. This was to instill in your mind the association that the values of facts were stored in this memory area. The term used for OPS5 fact memory is *working memory*, which is often abbreviated as *WM*; this is a memory area where the values of facts are stored. A single fact is called a *working memory element*. Working memory is accessed in the following ways:

- The user can store working memory elements during program coding.
- Rules can add, remove, or modify facts that are in WM during program execution.

- The inference engine matches rule patterns against WM elements.
- During debugging, the user can examine working memory using OPS5's interactive shell.

2.1.1 Structure of Working Memory

OPS5 allows the programmer to create data structures in the working memory. The reason that we must create data structures is two-fold:

- The programs that we write can have large amounts of facts, and if we do not structure these facts in a logical fashion, the programs will be difficult to conceptualize and debug.
- The OPS5 program, as well as the designer, must have an efficient way to access all the information in the working memory. For reasons of efficiency, the structure of the facts in each program must be presented to the inference engine before things are added to working memory.

The loan qualification example of Chapter 1 has been used to demonstrate the need and use of an OPS5 data structure. Declaration of working memory structure is similar to declaring structures or records in C or Pascal, except that OPS5 allows data of any type to go in a field, while C or Pascal restricts the assignments to the type that is initially declared. The following code shows how the information in the loan example might be structured in the OPS5 working memory using the OPS5 `literalize` command:

```
(literalize applicant name ss-num income savings debt)
(literalize loan-action disapprove approve)
```

The OPS5 language dictates a form in which all working memory must be represented. It is very clear and self-documenting as long as the designer makes the effort to logically represent the knowledge in the most natural way. The form is

```
(element-class attribute/value-pair-1 attribute/value-pair-2 ...)
```

The *element class* is essentially the name of the data type that is used by the OPS5 environment and the programmer. OPS5 requires a name to define an element class. A specific element class is identified by name when the data contained within the scope of the identifier needs to be accessed. Note that in the code above, element classes are identified as the first string that follows `literalize`. The dash (-) in `loan-action` must be used to link words because whitespace characters (tabs, spaces, and linefeeds) are used as separators in OPS5. In this example, `applicant` and `loan-action` are the two classes. Each class has a list of attributes associated with it and each attribute has a unique name. When using the `literalize` command, there are no values given, e.g., no number after `ss-num`, because this is a "template" for data but does not actually create any data. The values for the attributes will be assigned later. The terms *element*, *element class* and *class* mean the same thing and they will be used interchangeably throughout the book.

The OPS5 language requires that working memory elements must be declared (literalized) in the first section of any OPS5 program (i.e., before the first working memory can be made, all of working memory must be structured). The section that structures the working memory is called the *literalization* section. All the literalization section is doing is defining (declaring) the classes of data that the program will use. The code in the preceding section demonstrated how an OPS5 program would literalize WM. The literalization section sets up the OPS5 environment so that the working memory has the designated class-attribute templates available. These templates will be invoked as each class of data elements is used in the program. Keep in mind that the number of elements in working memory may increase and decrease as the program executes and there is no predetermined limit on the number of attributes contained in an element class (of course, the size of the memory of the computer you are using does eventually impose limits on working memory expansion). Examples of WM expansion and contraction will be demonstrated after it is made clear how values are given to attributes.

2.1.2 Initialization

Working memory is structured by the user in what is called the *literalization* section of an OPS5 program. This section creates WM "templates" that represent how each category and fact will be stored. The first action that usually occurs in an OPS5 program is the initialization of WM by dedicated rules whose sole purpose is to initialize WM (create facts in working memory). This creates a foundation of knowledge that will be accessed by the inference engine and the rules.

Now that the structure of working memory has been established, we must consider how to create values within this structure. OPS5 has a command that will create values in WM. The `make` command is used to create working memory elements. The following code demonstrates the use of this command in relation to the Loan Qualification example. But there are a few important points to be addressed since this code will be using the OPS5 interpreter. Each OPS5 interpreter will have a system-dependent procedure required to invoke it. The environment that is used for this book simply requires `OPS5` to be typed. Other versions might require the user to invoke LISP, then load the OPS5 code. When the OPS5 shell is in place it will print a message and a prompt, such as `:` or `>`. Readers should refer to the user's manual of their OPS5 interpreter for correct operating information. You may also refer to Appendix A for an example of how to use one particular OPS5 interpreter.

Working memory is initially cleared by the OPS5 environment when the interpreter is first loaded. The interpreter command `(WM)` will display the contents of WM, as demonstrated in lines 1 and 2 of Example 2.1. In this example, and in many others, we will use line numbers to make it easier to refer to specific lines. These line numbers do not appear in the actual OPS5 programs or in the output of the interpreter; in our examples they are only used for clarity. Note that because many OPS5 interpreters have been implemented in LISP, all commands must be enclosed in parentheses for OPS5 to recognize them.

Example 2.1. Examining working memory

```
1    : (wm)
2    Working memory is Empty
3    : (make applicant ^name john)
4    : (wm)
5    1:  (applicant ^name john)
6    : (make applicant ^name tom)
7    : (wm)
8    2:  (applicant ^name tom)
9    1:  (applicant ^name john)
10   : (remove 1)
11   : (wm)
12   2:  (applicant ^name tom)
13   : (make applicant ^name john)
14   : (wm)
15   3:  (applicant ^name john)
16   2:  (applicant ^name tom)
17   : (remove *)
18   : (wm)
19   Working memory is Empty
```

Now that the OPS5 interpreter is running, WM can be literalized and initialized. Note that if a value of an attribute is not known, it should be initialized to `nil`, the symbol for empty. This allows the program to check for WM locations that do not yet contain data. As in any other programming language, it is good programming practice to initialize all variables to known conditions at the beginning of a program, even though certain implementations might do this for you.

In line 3 of Example 2.1, we see how to enter an element in WM using the `make` command. Remember that statements following the OPS5 prompt (> or `:`) are user-entered commands.

The `make` command uses a previously literalized template and reproduces it with appropriate values added. Thus we can build (add to the contents of) WM by using the `make` command, as shown in line 6.

WM should be cleared before each program is loaded into the OPS5 shell because OPS5 leaves all the previously created values in WM. Even if you run the same program again, the WM area must be cleared. This allows you to generate a unique set of facts for each execution of a program. It is the responsibility of the user to clear WM whenever it is to be reused. If the working memory was not cleared, then all the previous fact values will still be present when you run the program, potentially creating erroneous results. The user can clear any working memory element from WM by using the `remove` command. The `make` and `remove` commands can be used in the interpretive mode (directly typed in by the user) or in the right-hand side of a rule (action taken when the rule is fired). Lines

10 and 17 of Example 2.1 demonstrate how the action command **remove** is used in the interpretive mode. Notice that **remove** can delete just one working memory element as in line 10, or remove them all, as in line 17.

As was demonstrated, the **make** command creates values in WM and the **remove** command deletes elements from WM. To change a value that has already been created in WM, a new command is needed: **modify**. The **make** command loads values into WM by actually creating new data structures, while **modify** only changes values in an existing working memory element. Line 4 of Example 2.2 demonstrates the **modify** command. Notice that the original instance of **applicant** with the name **john** has changed. You may think of **modify** as removing an old working memory element, and making a new modified working memory element with the time tags updated.

Example 2.2. Modifying working memory

```
1        : (wm)
2        2:  (applicant  tom)
3        1:  (applicant  john)
4        : (modify 1 applicant john-smith)
5        : (wm)
6        3:  (applicant  john-smith)
7        2:  (applicant  tom)
```

The **make** commands that initialize the working memory can be typed to the interpreter, as we have seen. This is not adequate for the very large databases that we often need in real expert systems; therefore, these **make** commands can be incorporated in the first rule fired by the OPS5 program. **Make** commands can also be used as separate lines of code that are not contained within the rules of the program. As lines of code outside the rules, the **make** works because the interpreter takes one line of code at a time and will execute the **make** on entry into the program.

The previous discussions and coding examples have demonstrated the way the WM is accessed in OPS5. The interpreter allows the user quickly to change values in WM and to see exactly what is contained in WM. Before any more can be said about WM, the structure and use of rules must be investigated. The power of a rule-based system is in having the rules access and change WM.

2.2 RULES

Rules are used in OPS5 to access the WM and to encapsulate the expertise of the system. The actions that they cause should eventually lead to a correct conclusion; therefore, the rules must be designed with a complete understanding as to exactly what the system should solve. The way the rules interact with WM is crucial to the operation of the system. Rules contain patterns that match WM and they can modify WM. Rules can call external routines and can build new rules. Rules are the workhorses of the rule-based system and it is very important that the system developer understand exactly how they work.

2.2.1 Structure of OPS5 Rules

OPS5 rules are structured as IF-THEN pairs where the IF section deals with matching patterns against existing facts and the THEN section is a list of actions to be taken:

```
IF   <certain patterns are true>
THEN <actions to be taken>
```

The pattern section of the rule will be designated by the term *left-hand side* (LHS) and the action section will be designated by the term *right-hand side* (RHS). It is common to use the abbreviations LHS and RHS when talking about OPS5.

The LHS deals exclusively with working memory as it attempts to determine if the specified patterns are true. The RHS deals with all areas of the OPS5 environment, including working memory manipulation, input and output, rule building, and calls to other languages.

A description of an OPS5 rule follows:

1. The rule is enclosed in parentheses:

```
( )
```

2. The letter `p` is always the first character to follow the left parenthesis, and means *production*:

```
(p  )
```

3. A rule's name is needed to identify the rule uniquely for the programmer as well as the OPS5 interpreter. This name can be as simple as `Rule1`, but to help make programs self-documenting, a meaningful description of what the rule does would be a better choice. The self-documenting technique helps us to understand the program as we design and debug it, but we must remember to change to a more meaningful rule name if the purpose of the rule changes. Our example rule will be used to initialize WM, so we choose the obvious name:

```
(p initialize-WM)
```

4. We now set up the patterns to be matched against working memory. There has to be at least one pattern in the LHS or the rule will never have a match and can never fire. Continuing with the example, a dummy class is used: `start`. This means that the only condition that the rule `initialize-WM` needs to allow it to fire is the existence of the class `start` in WM, and `start` does not need to have any attributes.

```
(p initialize-WM
   (start)
)
```

5. Since `start` is the only pattern that is included in the left-hand side, the next thing we add to the rule is the symbol `-->`. This symbol serves as a separator between the LHS and the RHS, and can be read as "then":

```
(p initialize-WM
   (start)
-->
                  )
```

6. Now we must determine what action is to be taken. In the following code, WM is to be initialized with the values for John Smith that were given earlier in this chapter.

```
(p initialize-WM
   (start)
-->
   (make applicant ^name John-Smith ^ss-num 04742997
         ^income  60000 ^savings  5000 ^debt 15000))
```

Example 2.3 is an example of how a rule is loaded into the OPS5 interpreter and run. The code for a rule must first be entered into a file using an editor. The **initialize-wm** rule was stored in the file **r1.ops**. The complete contents of the file **r1.ops** is presented below:

```
(literalize applicant name ss-num income savings debt)

(p initialize-wm
   (start)
-->
   (make applicant ^name john-smith ^ss-num 04742997
         ^income 60000 ^savings 5000 ^debt 15000))
```

The following sequence depicts how this file **r1.ops** is then loaded into the OPS5 environment and subsequently executed. Notice that you can display a rule by using the (`pm` *rule name*) command. See Appendix B for more information on OPS5 commands.

Example 2.3. A sample run of the OPS5 interpreter

```
OPS5> (load r1.ops)
      * Loading file R1.OPS ...
      * Production INITIALIZE-WM compiled.
```

```
OPS5> (pm initialize-wm)

      (p initialize-wm
         (start)
      -->
         (make applicant ^name john-smith ^ss-num 04742997
           ^income 60000 ^savings 5000 ^debt 15000))

OPS5> (wm)
      NIL

OPS5> (make start)

OPS5> (wm)

      1: (start)

OPS5> (run)

      1. INITIALIZE-WM : 1

      =>WM:  3 : ( APPLICANT ^NAME JOHN-SMITH ^SS-NUM 4742997 ^INCOME 60000
         ^SAVINGS 50000 ^DEBT 15000)

       end -- no productions true

OPS5> (wm)
       1 : ( START )
       2 : ( APPLICANT ^NAME JOHN-SMITH ^SS-NUM 4742997 ^INCOME 60000
          ^SAVINGS 50000 ^DEBT 15000)

OPS5>
```

Now the information for the other applicant (Tom Tucker) will be added to the rule. **r1.ops** will now contain:

```
(literalize applicant name ss-num income savings debt)

(p initialize-wm
   (start)
-->
   (make applicant ^name john-smith ^ss-num 04742997
     ^income 60000 ^savings 5000 ^debt 15000))
   (make applicant ^name tom-tucker ^ss-num nil
     ^income 40000 ^savings 25000 ^debt 100000))
```

The next sequence shows what would happen if one loaded the program above and ran it in the OPS5 environment that was used to run the first version. Notice that the commands (remove *) and (excise *) are needed to clear out the OPS5 environment before loading in another file. If this is not done, then extraneous rules and facts will still exist from previous programs, possibly causing the rules from the second program to match on working memory elements from the first.

```
OPS5> (remove *)

OPS5> (excise *)

OPS5> (load r1.ops)
      * Loading file R1.OPS ...
      * Production INITIALIZE-WM compiled.

OPS5> (wm)
      NIL

OPS5> (make start)

OPS5> (wm)
      1: (start)

OPS5> (run)
      1. INITIALIZE-WM : 1

      =>WM:  2 : ( APPLICANT ^NAME JOHN-SMITH ^SS-NUM 4742997 ^INCOME 60000
             ^SAVINGS 50000 ^DEBT 15000)
      =>WM:  3 : ( APPLICANT ^NAME TOM-TUCKER  ^SS-NUM NIL ^INCOME 40000
              ^SAVINGS 25000 ^DEBT 100000)

      end -- no productions true

OPS5> (wm)
      1 : ( START )
      2 : ( APPLICANT ^NAME JOHN-SMITH ^SS-NUM 4742997 ^INCOME 60000
              ^SAVINGS 50000 ^DEBT 15000)
      3 : ( APPLICANT ^NAME TOM-TUCKER  ^SS-NUM NIL ^INCOME 40000
              ^SAVINGS 25000 ^DEBT 100000)

OPS5>
```

Notice that a whole new applicant template containing Tom Tucker's information has been added to WM. This will occur for as many instances of applicant as need be; each applicant has a unique grouping of data.

To review, the basic structure of an OPS5 rule is simply:

```
(p
   LHS
```

```
    -->
      RHS)
```

The LHS and RHS can each have many statements and there can be as many rules in a program as are needed (the size of the program is limited only by the memory bounds of the machine that it is running on). Every rule must have at least one condition in the LHS (or it could never fire), at least one action on the RHS (or it would not do anything), and every rule's name must be unique (no duplicate rule names allowed).

The limits of typing rules directly to the interpreter are evident as the rules grow in size. In practice, programs are stored in files, which saves the programmer from retyping rules every time the interpreter is invoked. Therefore, for the rest of the book, we will assume that our OPS5 programs are stored in files and are loaded into the OPS5 shell by using the `(load "filename")` command, where `filename` is the name of the appropriate file. Refer to Appendix A for a complete discussion of OPS5 source files and how to use them. Note that semicolons (`;`) are comment symbols, which means that all text on a line following a semicolon is viewed as a comment for persons reading the program and is ignored by the interpreter.

2.2.2 Left-Hand Side

The LHS of a rule contains patterns that when matched, enable that rule to fire. These patterns are what the inference engine will use as it searches memory. When the inference engine cycles through the rules it looks at the LHS of each rule to try to match the LHS working memory patterns with the actual values in working memory. At first glance, this may seem very inefficient, but the matching is not done in the most obvious way. The actual way that the inference engine matches the LHS patterns is discussed in the chapter on the Rete algorithm, Chapter 6. For now, let us say that a complete match either is found or is not found in WM, and that a rule is fired only when a complete LHS match occurs. The loan qualification (LQ) example from Chapter 1 will be used to illustrate how the left-hand side can match working memory. The OPS5 program `LQ.OPS` will serve as the basis for all the rules discussed in this section. That means that WM will always be initialized in the same way. Rules can now be written to access the WM and solve problems that relate to the classes and attribute values. These rules can be added to `lq.ops` to create a working OPS5 program.

Simply stated, the LHS of the rule contains the patterns that relate to the action that the rule will perform. More important, the LHS must relate to the logic of the whole expert system. The flow of the problem-solving scenario is guided by the LHS patterns. The rules that were developed in Chapter 1 will serve as examples.

Rule1: This rule was put in to check if any fact information was incomplete. It only checks the social security numbers, but checks on all other facts could be performed. The left-hand side of this rule is set up so that it will check all the social security numbers of all the applicants in the WM. The OPS5 code for Rule1's LHS is as follows:

```
; rule to check all ss-nums
(p rule1
```

```
   (applicant ^ss-num nil)
-->
:
)
```

The action section of this rule has been left out and will be discussed when right-hand sides are discussed. This rule will find all instances of applicants without social security numbers, and should fire once for each instance. Notice the way that the LHS pattern is formed. The class `applicant` is first identified, then the attribute of the class is named. An attribute name is always preceded by the up arrow (^) symbol. The value that is to be compared (in this case *nil* follows after at least one "white space" character (space, tab, or carriage return). The pattern in this example will cause the inference engine to search memory for the class `applicant`. If this class is found, then the class will be searched for the attribute `ss-num`. If the attribute `ss-num` is found, then the value associated with the `ss-num` in WM is compared to the value specified in the rule: *nil*. If the value for `ss-num` in WM is *nil*, then this rule is ready to fire. The exact way the matching is performed is discussed in depth in Chapter 6.

Any number of attributes can be included in the LHS patterns, and any number of patterns can be present in the LHS of a rule. A slightly extended version of Rule1 shows how to specify exactly which applicant to check:

```
; check only john smith's ss-num
(p rule1
   (applicant ^name john-smith ^ss-num nil)
-->
:
)
```

Rule2: This rule checks for applicants who have income that is less than their debt and whose savings is also less than their debt (i.e., the applicant is not a good risk for a loan). This rule introduces new ways of checking relationships between facts in WM:

```
(p check-debt-disapprove
  (applicant ^debt <appl-debt> ^income < <appl-debt> ^savings < <appl-debt>)
-->
:
)
```

The first attribute reference in the pattern is used to bind a variable `appl-debt` with the value of the debt of the applicant. Variables are designated by angle brackets: < and >. The name `appl-debt` was used to give a bit more meaning to the rule and stands for "applicant's debt." One way to create a variable and assign it a value is to do it in the LHS in a pattern. Now the variable `appl-debt` will represent the value of the debt of the applicant that has been accessed by the LHS. In OPS5 the existence of a variable is limited in scope to the rule that it was created in and the variable will cease to exist when that rule is finished being used. Note that the number of applicants in WM can range from zero to as many applicants that have been made active by the initializing rule that created them. The inference engine will sequence through the WM looking for all applicants to apply to the patterns.

The second and third attribute references use the variable `appl-debt` to compare to the income and savings of the applicant. Note that the predicate operator used is the symbol <, which means LESS THAN. With one exception, OPS5 is the same as Pascal in the use of these symbols as predicate operators, and a complete list is given in Appendix C. The second and third attribute references tell the inference engine to check if the applicant's debt (assigned by the first pattern to the variable `appl-debt`) is less than the applicant's income and less than the applicant's savings. If both these checks are true, then the rule is ready to fire. In OPS5, conjunction (which means that all patterns must be true to satisfy the whole pattern) is implicit in the structure of the pattern. By including an attribute in the pattern, that attribute must now also be verified along with all other attributes contained in the pattern, if the pattern is to be matched. Each pattern in the LHS is also viewed in conjunction (i.e., they all have to be matched for the rule to fire). One of the challenges of writing OPS5 code is to be able to perform the disjunctive OR `(if A OR if B then C)` operation using LHS of rules. This will be discussed in examples later in the book.

Another form of conjunction and disjunction is in the way attributes are related in the patterns. For example, if the range of the debt were important, then `Rule2` might include a pattern like this:

```
(p check-debt-disapprove
   (applicant ^debt {> 10000 < 500000})
   (applicant ^debt <appl-debt> ^income < <appl-debt>
              ^savings < <appl-debt>)
-->
.
.
.
)
```

The first pattern uses the conjunction form for attribute values. This is signified by the brackets { } and simply means that the values contained within must all be matched. In the code above, the first pattern states that the debt must be in the range between 10001 and 499999. Any of the predicate operators from Appendix C can be used within these brackets. In some OPS5 implementations, it is important that the location of the blank spaces inside the brackets be strictly observed; otherwise, there is a possibility that the program will not run correctly. Note that the variable `appl-debt` has been placed in the second pattern. This was done so as not to confuse the reader when first using the conjunction brackets. It is possible to assign a variable and to perform conjunction at the same time. `Rule2` could be written like this:

```
(p check-debt-disapprove
   (applicant ^debt {<appl-debt> > 10000 < 500000}
              ^income < <appl-debt> ^savings < <appl-debt>)
-->
 .
 .
 .
)
```

Now the value of the attribute **debt** is not only checked for a range, but also assigned to the variable **appl-debt** within the range specified. The other way to look at a range is by using disjunction. **Rule2** could be written like this:

```
(p check-debt-disapprove
   (applicant ^debt << < 10000 > 500000>>)
   (applicant ^debt <appl-debt> ^income < <appl-debt>
              ^savings < <appl-debt>)
-->
 .
 .
 .
)
```

The double angle brackets **<<** and **>>** are used for disjunction. This checks the range of the value for the attribute **debt** to be less than 10000 or greater than 500000. Values between 10000 and 500000 inclusive will cause the first pattern not to match. A variable can also be assigned in a disjunction:

```
(p check-debt-disapprove
   (applicant ^debt << <appl-debt> < 10000 > 500000 >>
        ^income < <appl-debt> ^savings < <appl-debt>)
-->
 .
 .
 .
)
```

As with conjunction, the location of blank spaces is sometimes crucial and a missed space could generate errors.

Rule3: This rule checks to see if the applicant's financial situation is stable enough so that a tentative approval can be granted. The form of this rule is similar to **Rule2** but has one different aspect. The description of the rule from Chapter 1 shows the calculations being performed in the LHS. OPS5 does not allow this (i.e., computations can only be carried out in the RHS of a rule). Therefore, this rule was included to show that a level of preprocessing must be performed if complicated mathematical relationships are used in patterns. This is not difficult because all the programmer has to add to the original WM template for applicant are the template locations for the new facts that are to be used. In this case, we store these values for each applicant: **half-income-plus-savings** and **one-and-a-half-debt**.

Then the math is performed in a rule's RHS using the **compute** command. This will load correct values into the attributes of the working memory elements. If the new attributes were given the names **half-income-plus-savings** and **one-and-a-half-debt**, then the WM template for applicant could be literalized like this:

```
(literalize applicant name ss-num income savings debt
           half-income-plus-savings one-and-a-half-debt loan-status)

(literalize loan-action disapprove approve)
```

The way the values for these new attributes are loaded will be discussed in the section on right-hand sides. The patterns for **Rule3** can now be written as

```
(p check-debt-approve
   (applicant ^one-and-a-half-debt <appl-debt>
              ^half-income-plus-savings > <appl-debt>)
-->
:
)
```

The first pattern in the LHS of this rule assigns **appl-debt** with the value that had been initialized with **one-and-a-half-debt** for an applicant in WM. Then the second pattern checks to see if the applicant's **half-income-plus-savings** attribute value is greater than **appl-debt**. In other words, the LHS is checking to see if the applicant tentatively qualifies for a loan by checking if half the applicant's income plus savings is 50% greater than the applicant's outstanding debt. If the relationship is true, then the rule is eligible to fire.

The structure of the LHS of OPS5 rules is straightforward. The correct flow of the logic of the OPS5 program is tied directly to the way that the patterns are constructed in the LHS and the order in which the patterns are listed in the LHS. These and the more subtle aspects of rule formation will be investigated in future chapters. But first the total picture of the OPS5 rule operation must be fully described.

2.2.3 Introduction to the Rete Matching Algorithm

In this section, we introduce the matching algorithm used in OPS5. It is called the Rete algorithm and it is used by the inference engine to match the attribute values stored in memory to the attribute values presented in LHS patterns. Chapter 6, which includes an in-depth discussion on the Rete algorithm, should be read by readers who want to know the details of the algorithm. The discussion that follows gives enough insight into the Rete operation so that the average user can design efficient OPS5 rules.

Conceptually, when the inference engine starts a cycle it will look at the LHS of all the rules. The inference engine proceeds through working memory and matches against each LHS, adding rules to the conflict set unless it determines a non-match (pattern that does not match against working memory), which will cause the inference engine to ignore the rule in the current cycle. This scenario continues until it has checked all the rules in the program. The cycling is repeated as long as at least one LHS matches, which means that at least one rule can fire. When none of the rules match, the inference engine halts and returns control to the OPS5 top level.

If this approach is used, then it would take an inordinate amount of time for a cycle to match a large group of rules. For example, if there are 100 rules with an average of 5 patterns each, and 40 working memory elements, then 20,000 matches would have to be performed on each cycle. If there have not been many changes to the values in WM between cycles, then there is also a great deal of similarity in working memory from one cycle to the next. This would mean that the interpreter is performing needless repetitive matches of productions against working memory. For example, let's look at one of the rules we used in the preceding section:

```
(p check-debt-disapprove
  (applicant ^debt <appl-debt> ^income < <appl-debt> ^savings < <appl-debt>)
-->
 .
 .
 .
)
```

Do the patterns in the LHS have to be checked again, e.g., compared to the applicant's income, during every inference engine cycle if the income value has not been altered? Once this program gets past the initialization section, the income value remains fixed for the duration of the program. It is not efficient to check the patterns in this rule during every cycle. Remember that the LQ program that is being built has only three rules. In larger, more complicated programs, the designer must develop a design methodology where the alterations to WM are easily identified during rule construction.

The mechanism that OPS5 uses to increase matching efficiency described above is called the Rete algorithm. This algorithm allows the inference engine to avoid the inefficiency of repeatedly matching static LHS patterns by creating a matched data network. The Rete algorithm stores the previously matched LHS conditions in the network so that the inference engine can access it on the start of the next cycle. Thus if LHS conditions had been matched in a previous cycle and the values that were matched have not been changed by the rule that just fired, then the inference engine will be able to reuse all those previously matched LHS conditions without having to perform the whole matching process again (note that this works with the LHS as a whole and with the individual condition lines separately). This process saves time because the inference engine does not have to "start from scratch" at the beginning of each cycle to verify matches. The important words to note in this discussion are: *...and the values that were matched have not been changed....*

If any of the matched values have been changed, the previous match that was stored in the Rete network is retracted to the point where the changes occurred, and the inference engine must now attempt a new match from that point on. That is the simplified operation of the Rete algorithm. But there is one key point that a designer must be aware of that will help with efficient program operation. The Rete algorithm tries to build a tree network of "previously matched" patterns, as described above, for each rule that is accessed by the inference engine. This tree network builds down as patterns are matched, with the first pattern in the LHS of the rule as the initial tree node and all subsequent LHS patterns as sequential nodes farther down the tree. The crucial point is that all the subsequent nodes of the tree build down from the initial node. Therefore, if you alter the values that are used by the first pattern in the LHS of a rule, then the Rete tree of "previously matched" patterns is erased (i.e., the lower nodes of the tree become unsupported if the initial node is in a state of change). In other words, if the values used in the first pattern of a rule are changed, then the first pattern must be matched again and the whole tree is lost as the matching process repeats. This tree is erased even if all the subsequent patterns are still valid. To remedy this inefficient operation, the rules should be designed so that the patterns with values that are prone to change are located in the latter part of the LHS. This makes them lower in the "previously matched" tree and allows for most of the tree to be saved and reused even when changes occur. In fact, the whole tree, up to the node just before the changed value, is retained and the LHS of the rule is represented as "previously matched" up to the pattern with the changed value.

Therefore, the inference engine will run more efficiently if the designer takes care to place the more static patterns in the early part of the LHS while placing the more dynamic conditions in the later lines of the LHS. It may not be obvious to a person just starting out as to how to identify the difference between a static and a dynamic condition. A simple example of static and dynamic facts, related to the LQ program, would be that any pattern using a person's name is very static (names rarely are changed), while a pattern using a person's debt can fluctuate daily, e.g., heavy use of credit cards for major purchases. Given enough programming experience, the OPS5 designer should eventually be able to make the distinction between dynamic and static (constant) values.

2.2.4 Right-Hand Side

The LHS cannot directly change any values in WM. The only "action" that the LHS can perform is to bind temporary variables. The real action that takes place in an OPS5 program occurs after the LHS patterns have been matched to existing facts in working memory and the rule executes the actions on the right-hand side (RHS) of a rule. Some of the actions are OPS5 top-level actions, while others are OPS5 functions that can only be called within a rule. Here is a quick summary of the types of action that a rule can perform:

1. Actions related to working memory
   - `MAKE`. Initializes values into new WM templates
   - `MODIFY`. Changes values in existing WM templates
   - `REMOVE`. Deletes values and templates from WM
2. Actions related to input/output
   - `WRITE`. Outputs data (can be a string of characters and/or variables)
   - `ACCEPT`. Inputs a "word" of data, which can be a number or a symbol
   - `ACCEPTLINE`. Inputs one line of data

- DEFAULT. Designates the path of the input and output (most OPS5 shells automatically default to the terminal for input and output; the input or output must be redirected with this function in order to read from or write to a file.)

3. Actions related to file access
   - OPENFILE. Opens a data file and assigns a name to it that can be referred to later
   - CLOSEFILE. Closes a file
4. Miscellaneous actions
   - COMPUTE. Performs math operations
   - HALT. Stops the inference engine and program
   - BUILD. Creates a new rule during program operation
   - CALL. Accesses subroutines external to the OPS5 shell
   - GENATOM. Generates a new atom or a symbol
   - LITVAL. Returns a number that represents the logical location of an attribute in WM
   - BIND. Assigns a value to a variable
   - CBIND. Assigns a WM element to a variable
   - SUBSTR. Returns a substring of a data structure

In the following discussion we demonstrate the basic RHS actions that an OPS5 designer needs to understand to get started. The more complex functions will be discussed in later chapters as you become more proficient in OPS5 programming.

2.2.5 Actions Related to Working Memory

Remember from the previous discussions that the make action is used to initialize WM attributes after they have been literalized. The make command, however, cannot be used to change the values in working memory because it takes an existing template and loads values into it (i.e., the make command creates a new working memory element every time it is used). An example of RHS action make is demonstrated in the initialize-WM rule in Example 2.4.

Example 2.4. Rule to initialize working memory

```
(p initialize-WM
   (start)
-->
   (remove 1)
   (make applicant ^name John-Smith ^ss-num 04742997 ^street 25-Lovers-Lane
         ^city Fairfield ^state Ct. ^zip-code 06430 ^income 60000
         ^savings 50000 ^debt 15000 ^loan-status pending)
   (make applicant ^name Tom-Tucker ^ss-num nil ^street 5-Colony-Road
         ^city Danbury ^state Ct. ^zip-code 06430 ^income 40000
         ^savings 25000 ^debt 100000 ^loan-status pending))
```

If this rule were fired, then WM would look like this:

```
(applicant ^name John-Smith ^ss-num 04742997 ^street 25-Lovers-Lane
   ^city Fairfield ^state Ct. ^zip-code 06430 ^income 60000
   ^savings 50000 ^debt 15000 ^loan-status pending)

(applicant ^name Tom-Tucker ^ss-num nil ^street 5-Colony-Road
   ^city Danbury ^state Ct. ^zip-code 06430 ^income 40000
   ^savings 25000 ^debt 100000 ^loan-status pending)
```

There are two instances of the type `applicant` created by the two `make` commands in the `initialize-WM` rule. Notice that the `remove` command has been included in the rule. This command will delete the element `start` from WM (the class `start` is not in WM at the end of the program—see above). This is done to ensure that the `initialize-WM` rule will fire only once. Without a matched `(start)` pattern, the rule cannot fire again. Remember that this is the initialization rule and is used to initialize memory. After memory is initialized, this rule is not needed. The number `1` is used by the `remove` command to refer to the first pattern in the LHS.

If an attribute in the `applicant` WM element needed to be changed after being initialized, and the `make` command were the only command available to store the change, then the `remove` action command would also have to be used. The specific applicant working memory element must be deleted from WM. Now the `make` action would have to reinitialize the entire applicant element, including changes. To simplify making changes in WM, OPS5 incorporates the two commands (`make` and `remove`) into the single `modify` action. The `modify` action allows us to change the values in WM efficiently. The following code is a new rule that will modify the applicant Tom Tucker's zip code and the applicant John Smith's state:

```
(p change
   (applicant ^name Tom-Tucker)
   (applicant ^name John-Smith)
-->
   (modify 2 ^state Connecticut)
   (modify 1 ^zip-code 04650))
```

The number that follows each `modify` command relates to the WM element that is matched by that line in the LHS of the rule. The number `1` means the WM element that is matched in the first pattern in the LHS, while number `2` means the WM element that is matched in the second pattern in the LHS. Therefore, `(modify 1 ...)` pertains to the applicant whose name is `Tom-Tucker`, and his zip-code value stored in WM will be changed to `04650`. The `modify` command can work on any number of attributes that are contained in the pattern class it is associated with. If this rule is added to the LQ program and the program is subsequently run, the `remove` and `make` operations that are performed by the `modify` command can be seen.

When running OPS5, we might want to see what rules are firing and what changes are being made to working memory. This is especially true during the debugging stage. There are three levels of detail that one can see when using the OPS5 interpreter. These levels are controlled by the interpreter commands: `(watch 0)`, `(watch 1)`, `(watch 2)`, and `(watch 3)`. The `(watch 0)` level does not display anything other than output from the `write` actions. It is used primarily for finished, debugged programs. The `(watch 1)`, `(watch 2)`, and `(watch 3)` levels display varying levels of rule and memory interactions. To find out what watch level the interpreter is set to, type `(watch)`. The interpreter will respond with the number of the current watch level. It is recommended that the reader set the watch level with `(watch 3)` and run the LQ program with the rule above included. The `(watch 3)` level shows every time a working memory element is removed and made. Note that this occurs for each modify command in the rule `WM-change`. When the program is finished running, the command `(wm)` can be used to show how WM has changed. Another way of verifying that the `modify` command worked is by using the `pbreak` command. This allows the user to *break* the program (give control to the interpreter) after a specified rule is fired. See Appendix B for some examples of debugging.

The user should become familiar with the top-level interpreter commands because they are used extensively in the debugging of OPS5 programs. In this book we demonstrate debugging scenarios as much as possible, but as in any programming language, debugging skill comes with experience and practice.

The following code shows two more rules from the LQ program. Another rule from LQ will be discussed in the next section, on input/output.

```
(p check-debt-disapprove
   (applicant ^name <ntemp> ^debt <appl-debt>)
   (applicant ^income < <appl-debt> ^savings < <appl-debt>)
-->
   (modify 1 ^loan-status disapproved)
   (make loan-action ^disapprove <ntemp>))

(p check-debt-approve
   (applicant ^name <ntemp> ^dbt+dbt/2 <appl-debt>)
   (applicant ^inc/2+sav > <appl-debt>)
-->
   (modify 1 ^loan-status tentative)
   (make loan-action ^approve <ntemp>))
```

The following is a representation of WM after the LQ program is executed with the two rules above included. Notice that each rule "makes" a separate instance of `loan-action`.

```
OPS5> (wm)
      1 : ( START )
      2 : ( APPLICANT ^NAME JOHN-SMITH ^SS-NUM 4742997 ^INCOME 60000
           ^SAVINGS 50000 ^DEBT 15000)
      3 : ( APPLICANT ^NAME TOM-TUCKER  ^SS-NUM NIL ^INCOME 40000
           ^SAVINGS 25000 ^DEBT 100000)
      4 : ( LOAN-ACTION ^DISAPPROVE TOM-TUCKER )
      5 : ( LOAN-ACTION ^DISAPPROVE NIL ^APPROVE JOHN-SMITH )
```

2.2.6 Actions Related to Input and Output

Initially, OPS5 expects all input and output from a running program to be via the terminal. Remember that all output is performed with the `write` command, and all input is from `accept` and `acceptline`.

The `check-ss-num` rule in the LQ example searches the `applicant` working memory elements for any applicant whose `ss-num` has not been entered (is `nil`). On finding a `ss-num` of `nil` the rule needs to query the user as to what the associated applicant's `ss-num` is. The LHS of the rule was given as

```
(p check-ss-num
   (applicant ^ss-num nil)
-->
:
)
```

If the LHS matches, then that means that an applicant has been found to be lacking a social security number. But how can this rule identify the name of the applicant? The pattern in the LHS must be rewritten so that the applicant's name is associated with a variable during the match. This can be done by prompting the user for information using the `accept` command.

```
(p check-ss-num
   (applicant ^name <ntemp> ^ss-num nil)
-->
:
)
```

Now `<ntemp>` will hold the name of the applicant that is associated with the `ss-num` of `nil`. When a match occurs, the RHS of the rule must cause action that will query the user of the program as to what the `ss-num` is for the matched applicant. This can be done by giving the name of the applicant and asking for a `ss-num` in response. The following code is an example of how to use the `write` command to send text to the terminal:

```
(p check-ss-num
   (applicant ^name <ntemp> ^ss-num nil)
-->
   (write (crlf) | Missing Social Security Number|)
   (write (crlf) | Applicant's Name is | <ntemp>)
   (write (crlf) | Enter Social Security Number: |))
```

When this rule is fired for the applicant Tom Tucker, it will produce output to the screen that looks like the following:

```
Missing Social Security Number
Applicant's Name is Tom-Tucker
Enter Social Security Number:
```

Notice that the statement `(crlf)` was embedded in the `write` command. The `(crlf)` sent a carriage return and line feed to the terminal. The `write` action can output text (contained within the | | brackets) and the values of variables (placed outside the | | brackets). The whole `write` action is contained within parentheses.

The next RHS action that has to be taken is the input action (`accept` command). The `write` action has asked the user to input the `ss-num` of Tom Tucker. The next action line needed is the `(accept)` line. This will cause the OPS5 program to wait for input from the terminal. When input is entered (terminated by a return key), the word that was input is stored in a temporary buffer. There are only two ways the OPS5 program can access this data. One is by associating it with an identifier (variable name) and this is done by use of another action command, `bind`. The command `bind` will associate a variable name to data. In this case the data is in the input buffer (via the `accept` command) and this data gets bound to the variable `<intemp>` in the last line of the rule:

```
(p check-ss-num
   (applicant ^name <ntemp> ^ss-num nil)
-->
   (write (crlf) |Missing Social Security Number|)
   (write (crlf) |Applicant's Name is | <ntemp>)
   (write (crlf) |Enter Social Security Number: |)
   (bind <intemp> (accept))
:
)
```

The second method is to put the `(accept)` directly in the `make` action as follows:

```
(p check-ss-num-2
   (applicant ^name <ntemp> ^ss-num nil)
-->
   (write (crlf) |Missing Social Security Number|)
   (write (crlf) |Applicant's Name is | <ntemp>)
   (write (crlf) |Enter Social Security Number: |)
   (modify 1 ^ss-num (accept))
:
)
```

The first method is preferable in most cases, because the variable can then be used in other ways in the same rule.

The following code is an example of what the display interaction with the `check-ss-num` rule would look like when it is fired for Tom Tucker. The user typed in the social security number of 55045117 followed by the return key:

```
Missing Social Security Number
Applicant's Name is Tom-Tucker
Enter Social Security Number: 55045117
```

The last action that must be performed in the RHS is the association of the input data (55045117) to the correct applicant's `ss-num`. Remember that the variables created within a rule are limited in scope to that rule, and they cease to exist when the rule has finished firing. The input data that is stored in the temporary variable `<intemp>` must be placed in working memory or it will be lost. The action command that does this is the `modify` command. The `modify` command is used in the same way as described in the previous discussion on how action commands relate to WM. The following code shows how the `modify` command can be implemented in the `check-ss-num` rule:

```
(p check-ss-num
   {(applicant ^name <ntemp> ^ss-num nil) <appss>}
-->
    (write (crlf) |Missing Social Security Number|)
    (write (crlf) |Applicant's Name is | <ntemp>)
    (write (crlf) |Enter Social Security Number |)
    (bind <intemp> (accept))
    (modify <appss> ^ss-num <intemp>) )
```

When fired for Tom Tucker, this rule will query the user to input a social security number. The input number will be stored in WM as the value of applicant Tom Tucker's `ss-num` attribute. Notice that the `modify` command uses the variable `<appss>` instead of the number 1 (as described in the previous discussion on using the `modify` command). The variable `<appss>` is called a class variable and is assigned in the LHS by using the {...} brackets. The use of class variables is helpful as a self-documenting convention and to help prevent bugs. Though the reference number of each pattern line can still be used in the RHS, class variables are recommended and will be used in this book for all future coding examples.

2.3 SUMMARY

In this chapter we have shown the basic concepts of how an OPS5 program runs in the OPS5 environment. Working memory is the place where data is stored. The rules contain the expertise of the system and they can be thought of has having two parts:

- The left-hand side (LHS), where there are patterns that match working memory
- The right-hand side (RHS), which is responsible for all the action that takes place in the program

In the next chapter, we will learn how the rules can be used to control the flow of a program and how conflict resolution is performed.

2.4 PROBLEMS

1. Explain the difference between "working memory" and "working memory element."
2. What does the "literalization" section of an OPS5 program do, and why is it needed?
3. Set up a possible working memory element for the following types of data: automobile insurance claims, personal computer configurations, and medical checkups.
4. Using the working memory that was developed in problem 3, write a single rule for each of the following:
   - Determine if a computer needs a hard disk and if it also needs a controller. Adjust WM to reflect the addition of a controller or a hard disk.
   - Determine if a computer needs a color or monochrome monitor. Also make sure that the correct video card is included along with the terminal.
   - Determine what the memory requirements are for the computer and add memory if needed. Make sure that the memory is of the right speed (i.e., relative to how fast the CPU is running).
5. Explain the structure of an OPS5 rule. Explain the distinctions between the LHS and the RHS.
6. Why and when is matching performed in OPS5?
7. Adjust all the rules that were written in problem 5 so that they query the user for the information needed. Also display the results of the actions on the screen.

3

INTERMEDIATE CONCEPTS of OPS5

3.1 HOW RULES CONTROL PROGRAM FLOW

Control is the heart of rule-based expert systems. All the other topics are peripheral to the issue of control; the expert system program must solve the problem that it was designed to solve. The problem-solving scenario is related directly to the way the rules in the system are structured. The expert system designer can control the operation of the system by designing the rules to operate in the following way:

- Have the LHS look for the appropriate facts that will bring the system closer to the solution.
- Structure the action of the RHS of rules to adjust working memory so that the LHS of important rules will be matched and subsequently fired.

The logical conclusion of a well-planned strategy is that when there are no more matches between the LHS of all the rules in the program and stored WM values, then the problem is solved for the current status of the state space and a solution can be determined. (The term *state space* refers to all possible situations on the way to solving a problem.) To design a system that will reach a solution when no more rules can fire is easily theorized but can be a complicated task. Experience is the only effective way to gain the practical insight that is needed in developing correct and efficient control strategies.

The primary way that rules control program flow is by altering working memory. A basic example of this was demonstrated in the program LQ. If the program ran without the `initialize-WM` rule firing, then WM would be empty and none of the left-hand sides of any of the other rules would be able to match. The inference engine would find no production rule true and it would stop the program without firing a single rule. But as soon as the `initialize-WM` rule is fired, it loads WM with values that in turn can be matched by the LHS of the other rules in the program. Therefore, the RHS action of the `initialize-WM` rule was designed to initiate the problem-solving scenario of the LQ program, and this rule must be the first rule to fire in the LQ program. In the next section we explain how the LQ program was designed so that `initialize-WM` will always be the first rule to fire.

3.1.1 The First Rule to Fire

The first rule to fire in an OPS5 program is usually the rule that initializes WM. There may be special cases where this does not hold true, but the logic of a rule-based system demands that WM be initialized so that the rules of the program can fire. Conceptually, the contents of WM represent knowledge and the expert system cannot solve a problem if the knowledge is not present.

The loan qualification program was designed so that the first rule to fire is the initialization rule. When an OPS5 program is run, the inference engine tries to match all the left-hand sides of all the rules. In the LQ program, the `initialize-WM` rule is fired because it matches the class `start`, while all the other rules in the program cannot fire because they need the `applicant` class.

To start an OPS5 program, the designer must create an initial working memory element with a `make` command. We use the term "instantiate" to mean the act of loading values into working memory elements (note that this definition may differ from definitions found in other texts). The designer of the LQ program seems to have three choices for which class to instantiate initially: the `start` class, the `applicant` class, or both classes. But on closer analysis, there is really only one choice: the `start` class. This is because the `applicant` class has many attributes and instances (one for each applicant). The instantiation of the `applicant` class is a non-trivial task and must be done by a rule if the operation of the system is to be efficient. The argument above eliminates both the second and third choices of what to instantiate first.

The `applicant` class in the LQ program is instantiated only by the right-hand side of the `initialize-WM` rule, and the class `start` must be instantiated before the `initialize-WM` rule can fire. Notice that there are no attributes associated with the class `start`; it has only a class distinction. It is legal to have an empty working memory element (a class with no attributes) in OPS5, but it is usually used in special circumstances such as this one to allow the LHS of the `initialize-WM` rule to match with the element class `start` and nothing more specific. The instantiation of an empty class in OPS5 can be performed as a top-level `make` command or in a rule. In LQ, the instantiation is performed by `(make start)`, which follows the literalization section (see Example 3.1, line 6). The reason that the `make` line was put directly into the program was to save the user from having to type (make start) before each run of the program. The line (make start) instantiates the class start into WM even though it is not contained in a rule. Also notice that OPS5 allows the program to create the working memory element start without literalization since it has no attributes. Literalization is required at all other times. By executing (make start) this program has:

- Initialized the working memory element start
- Satisfied the matching requirements of the LHS of the initial rule: initialize-WM

No other rule can fire because the program did not make any other working memory elements (i.e., there are no other elements present in working memory for other rules in the program to match). The very first action command in the initial rule's RHS is to remove the start element from WM by using the command (remove <st>). The <st> variable is a class variable used to identify the class start (see Example 3.1, line 4). This performs the same action as (remove 1), but the use of a variable makes the program more readable and guards against errors that tend to occur when patterns are added to or deleted from the LHS. The initialize-WM rule cannot fire again because none of the RHS of the rules modify the start element class and the inference engine strategy states:

Example 3.1. Initial rule

```
1   (p initialize-WM
2      {<st> (start)}
3   -->
4      (remove <st>)
5      (make applicant ^name John-Smith ^ss-num 04742997 ....))
6   (make start)
```

If a rule is fired once when matching a certain set of working memory elements, it cannot be considered for firing again unless there is a change in the access tags of the exact working memory elements that matched that rule. If they are modified in any way, then the rule can become eligible to fire again.

The next action that the RHS of the initial rule performs is the instantiation of two templates of the class applicant. The initialized working memory will now allow the other rules that use the class applicant to attempt LHS matches when the next inference cycle occurs. This is an example of how the action of a rule can affect the control of program flow by manipulating WM.

3.1.2 Using the LHS to Control Flow

The preceding subsection described how to choose and fire the initial rule in the LQ program. The next consideration in rule-based program design relates to the order in which the rest of the rules should fire. The OPS5 designer has the ability to guide rule selection before the inference engine uses its conflict resolution strategies (these inference engine strategies will be discussed in the next section).

Example 3.2. Loan qualification program

```
Rule1:  (p check-ss-num
          {(applicant ^name <ntemp> ^ss-num nil) <appss>}
        -->
           (write (crlf)| Missing Social Security Number|)
           (write (crlf)| Applicant's Name is | <ntemp>)
           (write (crlf)| Enter Social Security Number |)
           (bind <intemp> (accept))
           (modify <appss> ^ss-num <intemp>))

Rule2:  (p check-debt-disapprove
           (applicant ^name <ntemp> ^debt <dtemp> ^income < <dtemp>
                      ^savings < <dtemp>)
        -->
           (make loan-action ^disapprove <ntemp>))

Rule3:  (p check-debt-approve
           (applicant ^name <ntemp> ^debt-plus-halfdebt <dtemp>
                      ^halfincome-plus-savings > <dtemp>)
        -->
           (make loan-action ^approve <ntemp>))
```

After the initial rule is fired in the LQ program, the three rules in Example 3.2 will now be able to access the instantiated class `applicant`. The facts in the LQ program have been chosen so that the left-hand sides of all three rules will match and they will all be put in the conflict set. Normally, only a subset of the rules in a system will match at one time, but there is no hard and fast rule for how many should match at one time; this all depends on the way the rules were designed to interact. The discussion on rule partitioning in Chapter 4 will elaborate more on how to limit the number of rules that can fire.

The current flow of the LQ program is:

- Initialize working memory with information on current loan applicants.
- Perform three operations on the current loan applicants (not in any specific order):
  1. Fill in missing social security information.
  2. Disapprove applicant requests.
  3. Tentatively approve applicant requests.

On closer analysis, the order of the three operations does make a difference because all missing information should be compiled before any evaluation of loan qualification can be performed. This is standard operating procedure for financial institutions and the LQ program should be changed so that the rule `check-ss-num` will fire before the other two rules in Example 3.2.

An easy way to fix this is to add a pattern to the rules `check-debt-disapprove` and `check-debt-approve`. The pattern has to check if the `ss-num` is still `nil` and since the LHS is looking for a match, reverse logic is used. The following code should be used:

```
(applicant ^name <ntemp> ^ss-num <> nil ^debt <dtemp>)
```

The <> symbol means *not equal*, so this pattern will match a working memory element of type `applicant` if the ss-num is anything but `nil`. At this point, the reader should be able to make the LHS changes that have been described and verify that the program works accordingly.

The discussion above demonstrates how the addition of selected patterns to the LHS of rules can control the order in which rules will fire. The implementing of these patterns, along with the appropriate altering of WM by the RHS of rules, is the problem-solving scenario of an OPS5 program.

3.2 CONFLICT RESOLUTION

The inference engine may find more than one rule that has its LHS matched, signifying that the rule is eligible to fire. But OPS5 allows only one rule to fire in a given cycle. The inference engine must discard all but the "best" rule and then the inference engine will fire that rule. The group of rules that are found to have their LHSs matched is called the *conflict set*. This means that the rules contained within this set are in conflict: each is eligible to fire and could be chosen as the best rule to fire. An important point is that the same rule can be in the conflict set a number of times simultaneously *with different working memory elements*. Each set of rule and matching data is treated as a separate entity in the conflict set, even if the same rule appears more than once. The inference engine uses a prescribed strategy to choose a rule from this set. Example 3.3 illustrates the conflict set for each cycle in the LQ program. A new conflict set is created at the beginning of each cycle of the inference engine. After the conflict set is established, the next step is for the inference engine to filter out the undesirable rules using one of two user-selectable strategies: LEX and MEA.

Example 3.3. The conflict set

Cycle	Conflict Set	Rule Fired
1	initialize-WM 1	initialize-WM
2	check-debt-approve 2 check-ss-num 3 check-debt-disapprove 3	check-debt-disapprove
3	check-debt-approve 2 check-ss-num 3	check-ss-num

4	check-debt-disapprove 4 check-debt-approve 2	check-debt-disapprove
5	check-debt-approve 2	check-debt-approve

- Briefly, LEX is a conflict resolution strategy where the inference engine follows four steps in evaluating the conflict set for the best rule to fire:
  1. Eliminate previously fired rules if they are matching the same working memory elements as when they fired.
  2. If rules remain, select rules with the most recent WM reference.
  3. If there is still a tie, select rules with most conditional tests.
  4. If there is still a tie, select a rule randomly.
- MEA is a similar conflict resolution strategy with one step added.

It is important to understand how these strategies work because they are the deciding factors as to if or when a rule will fire. Competent expert system designers will configure their rules to fit into the control strategy being used. This ensures efficient and correct operation of the expert system. The following sections will elaborate on the integral parts of conflict resolution.

3.2.1 Time Tags

Before conflict resolution can be fully discussed, the concept of time tags (sometimes referred to as *access tags*) must be explained. Time tags are numbers that are associated with working memory elements and these numbers signify when a specific working memory element was created or last modified. Example 3.4 shows the WM after the rule `initialize-WM` is run.

Example 3.4. Working memory with time tags

```
; (a) OPS5 code for initialize-WM rule:

(p initialize-WM
   {<st> (start)}
   -->
   (remove 1)
   (make applicant ^name John-Smith ^ss-num 04742997 ^income 60000
         ^savings 50000 ^debt 15000 ^halfincome-plus-savings 80000
         ^debt-plus-halfdebt 22500)
   (make applicant ^name Tom-Tucker ^ss-num nil ^income 40000
         ^savings 25000 ^debt 100000 ^halfincome-plus-savings 45000
         ^debt-plus-halfdebt 150000))

; (b) State of wm after initialize-WM has fired:

    3: (applicant ^name tom-tucker ^income 40000 ^savings 25000
```

```
          ^debt 100000 ^halfincome-plus-savings 45000
          ^debt-plus-halfdebt 150000)
      2: (applicant ^name john-smith ^ss-num 4742997 ^income 60000
          ^savings 50000 ^debt 15000 ^halfincome-plus-savings 80000
          ^debt-plus-halfdebt 22500)
```

Notice that applicants John Smith and Tom Tucker each have a number associated with their working memory element and that Tucker's number is larger because his working memory element was the last created in the action part of the `initialize-WM` rule. It is an important distinction that the location of the `make` or `modify` command in the RHS of a rule has an effect on the value of these numbers (i.e., the time tag numbers generated by commands that appear earlier in the RHS will be smaller than the time tag numbers generated by commands that appear later in the RHS). The numeric values in Example 3.4 represent the time tags that are associated with every working memory element. If an element is modified (by the `modify` command) or created (by the `make` command), then WM updates the time tag accordingly. The specific value of a number does not matter as much as its relative value. In fact, numbers are eliminated when a `remove` command is executed and not reused, so only relative values matter. Notice in the example that John Smith was given time tag 2 because the element `start` had already been given time tag 1 when it was created by the `(make start)` command. Also notice that the element `(start)` does not exist in WM because it was removed in the initial rule. The sequential order of time tags is not altered by a `remove` statement; the time tag number is completely eliminated from WM and all new time tag numbers continue to progress sequentially higher. In general, an element with a very low time tag signifies that it was created early and has resided a long time in WM without being updated. In contrast, an element with a higher time tag has been created or modified recently; in fact, the element with the largest time tag is always the last (most recent) WM element updated. The numbers associated with the rules in the conflict set (see Example 3.3) are the time tags of the elements that have been matched in the LHS of the rules. In Example 3.3 each rule accesses only one element, and therefore there is only one number associated with the rule. In most cases a rule will access more than one element and the conflict set will show more than one time tag number associated with a rule. The magnitudes of the time tags are used by the inference engine to determine which rule to fire. The logic behind this assumes that the element with the most recent time tag is the element that has the most vital information related to the problem being solved. In other words, if the program is trying to work out a problem, then it is focusing on the most pertinent information, as opposed to data that has not been used since the program started. The time tags point out to the inference engine what data is dynamic and changing. Thus the inference engine follows the flow of changes by using the time tags as guideposts. The designer of OPS5 systems must understand this concept and develop rules that interact with this flow. The rules should be set up so that they alter the appropriate WM classes in such a way that the inference engine will progress though the problem in a logical, orderly fashion (i.e., the WM classes that are most recently altered signify which rule is to fire next).

3.2.2 LEX Conflict Resolution Strategy

The LEX strategy is the default conflict resolution strategy of the OPS5 environment. It can also be set at any time by the OPS5 command `(strategy lex)`, which can be typed to the interpreter or put into the RHS of a rule. The LEX strategy is composed of four steps:

- Discard rules in the conflict set that have already fired on the same data. If a single rule is left, then fire it; otherwise, continue to the next step.
- Compare the pattern types used in all the left-hand sides of all the rules in the conflict set, looking for the rule whose patterns match the most recently altered WM class. This is done by arranging in descending order all the time tags related to the LHS patterns and then comparing all the time tags. Those rules whose LHS patterns match the working memory elements with the most recent time tags qualify to fire. (If a tie occurs, then the next most recent element used in the LHS is checked against all the rules in the conflict set.) If a single rule qualifies, then fire it. If ties occur, then eliminate all other rules from the conflict set, except for the ties, and continue to the next step.
- Compare the remaining rules for the specific number of conditional test performed by LHS patterns on attributes and/or variables. The logic behind this is that the more tests the LHS has, the more important the rule is. If a single rule is left, then fire it. If a tie in complexity occurs, then eliminate all other rules from the conflict set, except for the ties, and continue to the next step.
- If there is still more than one rule in the conflict set after the steps above have been taken, then the rule to be fired is selected randomly. Example 3.5 demonstrates how LEX works for two cases of conflict sets. In cases 1 and 2 the LEX strategy has arranged the time tags of the matched classes of a hypothetical conflict set of rules, in descending order starting with the most recent time tag. This ordering allows the LEX strategy readily to identify the most recent time tag and in the case of a tie, the next most recent, and so on. LEX will pick `Rule1` to fire in case 1 (note that the first time tags of `Rule1` and `Rule3` are tied at 7; therefore, `Rule1` is picked because time tag 3 is greater than 1). LEX will pick `Rule2` to fire in case 2.

Example 3.5. Time tags using LEX

```
Case 1 - LEX
 Time Tags Rule1    Time Tags Rule2      Time Tags Rule3
       7                  6                    7
       3                  4                    1
       1                  2
```

```
Case 2 - LEX
 Time Tags Rule1    Time Tags Rule2      Time Tags Rule3
        5                  9                    8
        2                  1                    7
        1                                       5
```

3.2.3 MEA Conflict Resolution Strategy

The means-ends analysis, or MEA, strategy can be invoked by the OPS5 command `(strategy mea)`. Since MEA is not the default strategy, one of these methods must be chosen, or OPS5 will use LEX. The MEA strategy has five steps (note that the first step and the last two steps are the same as LEX):

- Discard rules in the conflict set that have already fired on existing data. If a single rule is left, then fire it; otherwise, continue to the next step.
- Compare the pattern types used in the first pattern line and only the first pattern line in the LHS of all the rules in the conflict set, looking for the rule whose first pattern line accesses the most recently altered WME. This is done by comparing all the time tags of the working memory elements that the first LHS patterns use. The rule whose first pattern matches the WME with the most recent time tag qualifies to fire. If a single rule qualifies, then fire it. If a tie occurs, then eliminate all rules except for the ties from the conflict set and continue to the next step.
- Compare the pattern types (from the second pattern on) used in all the rules in the conflict set, looking for the rule whose patterns access the most recently altered WME. This is done by arranging in descending order all the time tags related to the LHS patterns starting at the second pattern, and then comparing all the time tags. The rule whose LHS pattern accesses the WME with the most recent time tag qualifies to fire. If a tie occurs, then the next most recent WME used in the LHS is checked. If a single rule qualifies, then fire it. If ties occur, then eliminate all rules from the conflict set except for the ties, and continue to the next step.
- Compare the remaining rules for the specific number of conditional test performed by LHS patterns on attributes and/or variables. The reasoning is that the more tests in the LHS, the more important the rule is. If a single rule is left, then fire it. If a tie in complexity occurs, then eliminate all rules from the conflict set except for the ties and continue to the next step.
- If there is still more than one rule in the conflict set after the steps above have been taken, then perform a random selection to determine which rule to fire. Example 3.5 demonstrates how MEA works for two cases of conflict sets. In cases 3 and 4 the MEA strategy has sorted the matched working memory elements of a hypothetical conflict set of rules, in descending order starting with the *second* most recent time tag. It leaves the first time tag in its original state. This is the main difference between LEX and MEA (see Example 3.5). The order in case 3 is the same as in case 1. In other words, the order in which the patterns access the classes is taken to be naturally descending. Thus it is still a tie between `Rule1` and `Rule3`,

and the next level of time tags must be examined which gives the same result as LEX. In case 4 the natural order is assumed to be different from ascending, and `Rule3` will fire because it now has the most recent time tag in its first position. MEA differs from LEX in that the time tag of the class that the first pattern of a rule matches is the initial factor that determines which rule will fire. Thus the first pattern in the LHS of a rule has a very important control function in the MEA strategy.

Example 3.6. Time tags using MEA

```
Case 3 - MEA
  Time Tags Rule1      Time Tags Rule2      Time Tags Rule3
        7                    6                    7
        3                    4                    1
        1                    2

Case 4 - MEA
  Time Tags Rule1      Time Tags Rule2      Time Tags Rule3
        2                    1                    7
        5                    9                    8
        1                                         5
```

3.2.4 Choosing a Conflict Resolution Strategy

The main difference between the two conflict resolution strategies is that the LEX strategy is a simpler technique in which the order of the patterns does not matter, while the MEA strategy allows the designer to group rules into "modules." Modules help manage complexity in a program, and this will become more apparent with OPS5 programming experience (see Chapters 4 and 5). In the first section of this chapter we discussed how the LHS can be made to control the flow of the program. That was an example of external control by direct rule manipulation. The MEA strategy allows internal control through indirect rule manipulation.

The MEA strategy enables the designer to section off groups of rules and designate them to match a certain WME type at specific times. In other words, a program can activate a group of rules just by accessing a certain WME, making the time tag of that element the most recent. Conversely, the program can deactivate other groups of rules by not accessing a working memory element for a while. The MEA strategy will (with properly designed rules) help to reduce the size of the conflict set and the time it takes to fire rules. This will be discussed further in Chapter 4, in the section on rule partitioning techniques. The activation or deactivation of rules because of their time tags is dynamic, as opposed to the static manipulation of the LHS that was discussed at the beginning of this chapter.

There is one subtle point that must be made about the first sequence of both strategies: discarding rules that have already fired. The inference engine considers a rule to have been fired if it is a rule that was selected from the conflict set and whose

RHS actions were executed. What is not obvious in this definition of a fired rule is that the rule was fired because the rule's LHS patterns matched with WM classes that had the most recent time tags. As long as the time tags that are specific to the fired rule remain dormant (all the WM elements used by the LHS patterns are not modified), then the inference engine will discard the fired rule from the succeeding conflict sets. But if any of the working memory elements that the LHS of the fired rule had matched are modified, yet still match the LHS conditions, then the inference engine must include the rule in the next conflict set because the rule has new potential (i.e., new values in WM to match patterns with). In other words, if the element classes used by the patterns in the LHS of a rule are updated after the rule has been fired, then the time tags are updated also. This means that the values that the patterns in the LHS are trying to match may be different (i.e., they have been updated) from the values that caused the match that previously fired the rule. This will cause the Rete network to be altered and the rule is eligible to be fired again. In simpler terms, if any of the values of a WME are modified in any way, a rule that uses that WME becomes eligible to fire no matter how many times that rule has fired before. This is how rules move back and forth between the conflict resolution categories of *fired* and *conflict set.* A control problem that arises from the interaction above is the possibility of an infinite loop occurring. For example, if a rule's RHS action command modified all the classes that the LHS has used to match its patterns, then the time tags of those classes would be the most recent and it is possible that this one rule might continually enable itself forever (until you stop the program). Example 3.7 illustrates an example of a rule that would get into an infinite loop if it was used in the context of the LQ program. Understanding the cause of infinite loops can help the designer to avoid the problem.

Example 3.7. An infinite loop in OPS5

```
1    (p loop-infinite
2      {(loan-action) <la>}
3     -->
4      (modify <la> ^disapprove nil ^approve nil))
```

The rule in Example 3.7 will fire when the LHS pattern matches and the time tags are the most recent. The rule will change the `loan-action` attributes by using a `modify` command. This seems to be simple enough, but remember that when an element is modified, the time tag is updated. And in this case, the class `loan-action` will have the most recent time tag. The rule will be eligible to fire again because the update of the time tag of the class `loan-action` (caused by line 4) tells the inference engine that the patterns in the LHS of this rule have been changed. Therefore, this rule will constantly modify the `disapprove` and `approve` attributes of the class `loan-action` in WM. And in the process, it will make itself eligible to fire again and again. One fix for an infinite loop is to use more than one pattern and make sure that the rule does not modify all of the classes that are used in its LHS.

3.2.5 Demons

Demons are rules that are meant to fire at a certain point in a program no matter what other rules are in the conflict set. This could be to handle some extraordinary condition, or just to keep the system from stopping. An example of a demon is the initial rule (`initialize-WM`) in the LQ program. As long as the element class `start` is initialized by `(make start)`, then the demon `initialize-WM` must fire. A common use of the demon is as a "catchall" rule that fires when all others fail. It can generate an error message, take emergency action, clean up working memory, or take control of the logical flow of the program. When and whether a demon is fired is subject to the conflict resolution strategy that is used and to the extent that other demons in the system are competing for selection. The demon can be used as an effective control element, making sure that the program will perform vital operations. Example 3.8 shows how an "exit" demon can be put into the LQ program. An exit demon is a rule that will always be the last rule to fire before the program stops. It can be used to tie up loose ends or transfer control. In this case, the demon simply prints a message that the LQ program is finished. The reason that this rule is the last to fire is because one of the working memory elements used by the LHS patterns was the first created in WM (see Example 3.8) and thus had the lowest time tag. The class `demon-test` which is used in the LHS of the demon rule, was purposely created first (see Example 3.8, line 2) in the RHS of the `initialize-WM` rule to ensure that the class `demon-test` would have the lowest time tag (see Example 3.8).

Example 3.8. A demon to halt the program

```
; Add the following code to the literalization section:
        (literalize demon-test)

;Add to the following to the right hand side of initialize-WM:
   -->
1      (remove <st>)
2      (make demon-test)
         .
         .
         .
; State of WM after the initialization rule is fired:
 1  4: (applicant ^name tom-tucker ^income 40000
 2         ^savings 25000 ^debt 100000 ^halfincome-plus-savings 45000
 3         debt-plus-halfdebt 150000)
 4  3: (applicant ^name john-smith ^ss-num 4742997
 5         ^income 60000 ^savings 50000 ^debt 15000
 6         ^halfincome-plus-savings 80000 ^debt-plus-halfdebt 22500)
 7  2: (demon-test)

   (d) Add new rule:
     (p demon-end-program
         {(demon-test) <dt>}
     -->
```

```
(remove <dt>)
(write (crlf) |The LQ Program is finished.|))
```

3.3 ARITHMETIC OPERATIONS

OPS5 can perform standard arithmetic operations such as multiply (*), add (+), subtract (-), division (//), and modulus (\\). The RHS command `compute` is used to invoke these operations. If a program needs more complicated math functions, the best approach would be to use an external call to a language better suited for math operations. The results can be passed back as arguments or files (see Chapter 7 for a discussion of external calls).

3.3.1 Using Arithmetic Actions

Arithmetic operations must take place in the RHS of rules. The OPS5 command for arithmetic is `compute`, and it needs at least two arguments separated by an operation. The arguments can be numbers (constants) or variables. The variables are given values that relate to WM attributes and the result of the computation is usually stored in WM. For example, the `initialize-WM` rule can be rewritten so that the rule will determine the `half-income-plus-savings` and the `debt-plus-half-debt` attributes (remember that these attribute values are now precomputed before the `initialize-WM` rule is coded and the values are hard-coded into the source code of the rule). Example 3.9 represents the new version of a rule using the `compute` command. This version of the `initialize-WM` rule puts the burden of mathematical computations onto the computer.

Example 3.9. Using the compute action

```
(make start)

(p initialize-WM
   {<st>(start)}
-->
   (remove <st>)
   (make demon-test)
   (make applicant ^name John-Smith ^ss-num 04742997
        ^income 60000 ^savings 50000 ^debt 15000
        ^half-income-plus-savings (compute ((60000//2)+50000))
        ^debt-plus-half-debt (compute (15000 + (15000//2))))
   (make applicant ^name Tom-Tucker ^ss-num nil ^income 40000
        ^savings 25000 ^debt 100000
        ^half-income-plus-savings (compute ((40000//2)+25000))
        ^debt-plus-half-debt (compute (100000+(100000//2))))
```

Notice that the value of `half-income-plus-savings` and `debt-plus-half-debt` have been replaced by the `compute` command with its arguments and operations.

The OPS5 compute operations are performed starting from the right. The value of the arguments will be evaluated before the make command is executed. The compute command can have as many operations and arguments as needed. The parentheses are used in this example to separate the arguments so that readability is maintained. They can also be used to change the order in which the operations are performed (i.e., the operations inside the parentheses are performed first).

3.3.2 Interaction with WM

Example 3.9 demonstrates how the RHS can perform arithmetic in OPS5. The values used in this case are constants and will not change unless the programmer edits the program. Therefore, the use of a compute in the initialize-WM rule is only slightly better than the previous version of the initialize-WM rule. The next section on files will show how a general version of initialize-WM can be built. But first, the way that the compute command can access WM must be discussed.

If a rule was supposed to perform an arithmetic operation on a value in WM then it would have to access the value by using a pattern on the left-hand side of a rule. Then the rule would be able to perform the math in the right-hand side and modify the attribute. For example, a rule that would change the value of the income attribute in the class of applicants to "tax-adjusted income" might look like the rule in Example 3.10. This code subtracts 30% of the applicant's income from the original income figure and changes the WME. Notice that the only way to access the stored value for income is to use the rule variables <tincome> and <tapp>. The variable <tincome> is an attribute variable that contains the value of the income attribute and the variable <tapp> is a class variable that holds the location of the specific applicant class that is being accessed. It is important to note that this rule will loop and adjust all the incomes of all the applicants in WM because no specific applicant name was included in the LHS.

Example 3.10. Calculating after-tax income with compute

```
(p income-adjust
  { (applicant ^income <tincome> ) <tapp>}
  -->
  (modify <tapp> ^income (compute (<tincome>-(<tincome>*.30)))))
```

The compute command can be used effectively to perform simple arithmetic operations. The requirement that the compute command has to be located in the RHS of a rule presents design problems. First of all, LHS patterns that need to use mathematically derived WM values must be planned ahead of time. Remember that the LHS cannot do the math. The designer must be sure that the derived values have been computed and stored in WM before the rules that will use them can be fired. This could be done via a special rule designed just to perform the computation (as was demonstrated above).

Example 3.10 represents a simple fix that could be used as long as the number of rules allowed in a system is not a design constraint (i.e., new rules have to be added to the system). Using a specific rule to handle the math is a less complex approach and causes fewer bugs. A more complex approach is to perform the math as an extra RHS line in a rule that is routinely accessing the required class. This is tricky and can lead to logic flow problems. Another design issue is whether to store the computed values back in the original attribute location (thus writing over the original data and losing it) or to use a temporary memory location (add more class attributes to WM). As the needs for temporary storage locations arise, it is prudent to review the contents of WM and develop the best approach to handling these needs.

Any time that a `modify` command is used, it changes the time tag of the class that it is modifying. Therefore, if computations are being performed and stored in WM, the designer must be constantly aware of the order of occurrence of the modifying rules. The types of computations can alleviate some of the problems. If the computation is of a static nature and can be performed as an initialization procedure, then the best approach is to do the computation early in the program. The `initialize-WM` rule in Example 3.9 and the rule in Example 3.10 are examples of computation in rules that perform computations on dynamic data (data modified during the running of the program). They are more complicated to implement and must adhere to the strategy of the whole problem-solving system. For example, questions that might be asked by the designer are:

- Will the data be ready for a specific computation?
- What other rules will also be in contention to fire along with the computation rule?
- What rules will be enabled to fire as a result of the computations?

3.4 BULK DATA OPERATIONS

One of the most powerful things about a computer is the way it handles large amounts of data. It is foolish to put a great deal of time into program development if the program cannot be applied to large amounts of generalized data. So far the LQ program has been made to work on two sets of data: two unique applicants. The first problem with the way that the `applicant` classes are being instantiated in LQ is that the initial values are hard-coded into the `initialize-WM` rule. If the values had to be changed, then the rule would have to be rewritten. The values are constant to this specific rule and lock the program into one specific problem-solving scenario: loan qualification of John Smith and Tom Tucker. In a real system, the values of a data class would be dynamic and might have to be updated. These updates have to be stored so that they can be used later in a problem-solving scenario that reflects the current trends of the problem.

The second problem with the way the `applicant` classes are being instantiated in the LQ program is with the number of data and applicants. It stands to reason that a loan company will have many more than two applicants. There must be a better way of initializing the data than by recoding the initializing rule for each applicant.

A third problem with the LQ program is the way the `loan-action` class is used to store the names of processed applicants. As the number of applicants grows, a structure must be used that will allow for searching, sorting, and storing of related groups of data.

3.4.1 File Access

Data files are usually the best way to store and retrieve large amounts of data in a computer system. The OPS5 language has facilities for files that are similar to those found in most modern programming languages. The typical scenario for file access is:

1. Open the file for reading or writing.
2. Read data from or write data to the file.
3. Close the file.

The LQ program will be used again as an example of how to use OPS5 data files. The applicant information will now be stored in a data file rather than in the `initialize-WM` rule. This allows for generalization of the data and the program. We now develop a version of the LQ program that reads its data from a file. The LQ program was initially designed to analyze three aspects of an applicant's data:

- If a social security number was present for the applicant
- If the applicant could be immediately disapproved
- If the applicant could be tentatively approved

The analysis above was performed concurrently on two applicants and only two applicants. If the number of loan applicants is increased, a design question of how many applicants to process at a given time is raised. Should the program create a working memory element for every applicant in the loan company's database and try to perform the evaluations concurrently, or should the program be run for one applicant at a time? The factors to consider in answering this question relate to the size of memory that is required to load the whole database, the number of applicants currently in the database, and the type of a program interaction expected (batch or interactive). There is no correct answer to this design question but most likely a compromise would serve as a starting point if specific constraints are not known. In the case of the LQ example, the approach we take is to open a file and process one applicant at a time until all applicants have been taken care of. This will be more efficient with respect to memory usage and the speed of processing individual applicants because of the limited number of applicants at this point. With larger numbers of applicants the program might be divided between real-time interaction (checking for complete data information such as the social security number) and batch (overnight processing of the approval status).

Now that a specific strategy has been chosen, the next task is to define what the data file will look like. The data corresponds to the structure of the class `applicant` and the values that were created in the rule `initialize-WM`. Example 3.11 gives a representation of the data for John and Tom. This was the data that rule `initialize-WM` in LQ used. Example 3.11 gives a representation of the same data in a data file called LQ.DAT. This data can be entered with an editor, or can be written by another program. The words of data are separated by blank spaces. Notice that the each grouping of applicant data is separated by the word `continue` and that the last word is `stop`. These words were arbitrarily chosen and are used as delimiters for the LQ program because the program must have a way of knowing when it has finished with the last applicant's data. This also allows the LQ.DAT file to grow and shrink without affecting the operation of the LQ program. There are, or course, many other possible ways to delimit records in a file.

Example 3.11. Using a data file

Data:

Loan Qualification data		
name	John-Smith	Tom-Tucker
ss-num	04742997	nil
income	60000	40000
savings	50000	25000
debt	15000	100000
half-income-plus-savings	80000	45000
debt-plus-half-debt	22500	150000

Contents of data file LQ.DAT :

```
John-Smith   04742997  60000 50000   15000   80000  22500 continue
Tom-Tucker   nil 40000 25000 100000 45000  150000 stop
```

The `initialize-WM` rule must be rewritten to access the LQ.DAT data file and load the applicant values into WM. The OPS5 command for opening a file is:

(`openfile` *access-name filename direction*)

In the example that we are developing, the access name is `appdata`, the filename is `LQ.DAT`, and the direction is `in`. The direction is either `in` or `out`, depending on whether the file is being read in or written out. The access name is the name that will be used by the program when referencing that specific file and it is a global reference that will be removed only when the file is closed. This is the only type of global variable that exists in OPS5. In this case the access name `appdata` was chosen. The command to open the LQ.DAT file in the LQ program is: `(openfile appdata |LQ.DAT| in)`.

The location of this command must be considered in relation to the rest of the program. In this case, it can be put into the `initialize-WM` rule or it can be put into a separate rule by itself. The logic of the program states that the initialization rule will be accessed over and over as each new applicant's data is input. If the data file is opened in this rule, then it would be opened again, and again. It is not correct programming procedure to try to open a file that is already open, so the `openfile` command will have to be put into a separate rule. The file could be closed and then opened again, but this would always reset the file pointer and start the file access from the very beginning. Therefore, the program would never reach all the data in the file. The sequential aspects of the data file are discussed in the following sections. The rule to open the file would look like this:

Example 3.12. A rule to open a file

```
(p open-data-file
  {(start)<st>}
-->
   (remove <st>)
   (openfile appdata |LQ.DAT| in)
   (make start2))
```

Notice that the pattern (start) has been moved from the initialize-WM rule to the LHS of the open-data-file rule. Once the file is opened, the data can be accessed by using one of three OPS5 commands: the accept or acceptline command, or the write command. Note that the OPS5 default "file" is the terminal, and this is why these commands worked for terminal I/O in previous chapters. If these commands include a valid file name, then the commands will use that file instead of the terminal. For example, (accept appdata) will read in one word from the LQ.DAT file that was set up in the preceding openfile command.

Each file has a pointer associated with it and this pointer points to the first symbol or word in the file when the file is opened (a symbol in OPS5 means letters and numbers that are separated by blank spaces). Each accept command increments the pointer to the next symbol in the case of an accept, or the next line in the case of an acceptline. The pointer can only be reinitialized (reset) when the file is opened again. The process just described is called sequential access because the pointer moves through the file sequentially. There is not random access to records in the file as there are in some languages.

Now the initialize-WM rule can be rewritten to make use of files. The make command is used with the accept command to initialize WM. The new initialize-WM rule is in Example 3.13. The literalization section must be updated to include the class more-data. The following code would have to be added: (literalize more-data delimiter).

Example 3.13. Using accept with a make

```
(p initialize-WM
   {<st> (start2)}
-->
   (remove <st>)
   (make demon-test)
   (make applicant ^name (accept appdata) ^ss-num (accept appdata)
         ^income (accept appdata) ^savings (accept appdata)
         ^debt (accept appdata) ^halfincome-plus-savings (accept appdata)
         ^debt-plus-halfdebt (accept appdata))
   (make more-data ^delimiter (accept appdata)))
```

When this rule is fired, the make command uses the file access variable appdata. This variable was bound to the LQ.DAT file when it was used as an argument in the open command in the `open-data-file` rule. The pointer for this file was automatically set to the first location in the data file LQ.DAT. As each `accept` command is reached, the data that the file pointer is pointing to is read and the file pointer is incremented to point to the next piece of valid data in the file. For example, if the file pointer in the LQ.DAT file was pointing to the first symbol, then after the line `^name (accept appdata)` is performed, the attribute `name` would have the value `john-smith` and the file pointer will be pointing to the next symbol, which contains the social security number. After the line containing `^ss-num (accept appdata)` is performed, the attribute `ss-num` will have the value 04742997 and the file pointer will be pointing to the place that contains John's income. This continues until all of the `accept`s have been performed.

The RHS of the rule in Example 3.13 can be rewritten to so that the attribute values of `halfincome-plus-savings` and `debt-plus-halfdebt` can be computed at the time of instantiation instead of being preprocessed before the data file is loaded. First the file LQ.DAT must be changed to use the new computation. Example 3.14 presents the new data file. Notice that the values for income, savings, and debt have been placed at the beginning of each grouping of an applicant's data. This is done because these values are needed for the computations of `halfincome-plus-savings` and `debt-plus-halfdebt` and must be stored in temporary variables. Therefore, they must be input first to allow for a whole `applicant` class to be instantiated with `make`. In Example 3.15, the `initialize-WM` rule has been rewritten so that the values for income, savings, and debt are loaded from the data file into variables by the `bind` command. Then the `make` is performed using these variables to compute the information needed and to initialize the correct values into WM.

Example 3.14. A new data file

```
Data File LQ.DAT:
60000 50000 15000 John-Smith 04742997 25-Lovers-Land Fairfield
Ct. 06430 pending continue 40000 25000 100000 Tom-Tucker nil
5-Colony-Road Danbury Ct. 06430 pending stop
```

Example 3.15. New RHS for initialize-WM

```
      .
      .
      .
  -->
   (remove <st>)
   (make demon-test)
   (bind <tincome> (accept appdata))
   (bind <tsavings> (accept appdata))
   (bind <tdebt> (accept appdata))
   (make applicant ^name (accept appdata)
      ^ss-num (accept appdata) ^income <tincome>
      ^savings <tsavings> ^debt <tdebt>
      ^halfincome-plus-savings (compute ((<tincome>//2)+<tsavings>))
      ^debt-plus-halfdebt (compute (<tdebt> + (<tdebt>//2))))
   (make more-data ^delimiter (accept appdata)))
```

In the `initialize-WM` rule that was developed in Chapter 2, the applicant's data had to be preprocessed for `halfincome-plus-savings` and `debt-plus-halfdebt` before the expert system could use the data. The rule in Example 3.15 is a rewrite of the `initialize-WM` rule and it incorporates the `compute` function that lets the program become more general: Only raw data is needed to run the program.

Now that the LQ program uses a data file it will be called LQ-FILE. When LQ-FILE is run and the `(make applicant ...)` command of the rule `initialize-WM` is finished, the WM `applicant` class will be initialized with John Smith's data and the file pointer will be pointing to `continue` in the data file LQ.DAT. The program will then analyze the data and make a decision as far as `loan-action`. But what about Tom's data? Notice that a new class `(more-data)` was used in the rule (see Example 3.15, line 11) and it is instantiated with the value of the delimiter in the data file; it will be either `continue` or `stop`. Demons must be added to check these delimiters. The `(make demon-test)` and `(make more-data)` are classes that will be used for control of the file input. The `demon-test` class was used previously to fire a rule and print out a message. Now it must be rewritten to determine when to close the file that is open. The class `more-data` is used with the class `demon-test` to tell when the file has been completely read. Demon class rules must do the following checks and action:

- If the delimiter is `stop`, then all the data has been accessed; close the file, display the results, and stop the program.
- If the delimiter is `continue`, then more data is available; modify or clear WM and restart the program.

These demons must always be the last rules to fire, so a special class `(demon-test)` has been literalized and it will be the very first class instantiated in the `initialize-WM` rule (thus it will have the least recent access tag). The code in Example 3.16 represents the demons to be used. The demon in Example 3.16(a) will fire if the class `demon-test` and the class `more-data` are the classes with the most recent access tags and the delimiter in the class `more-data` is `stop`. Therefore, it will fire only when the access tag of `demon-test` is the least recent in relation to all other access tags. Notice in Example 3.16(a), line 6, that the command `closefile` is used with the access name of the file. It is always important to close an open file before ending a program. Another action taken in Example 3.16(a), lines 7 and 8, is the printing of the names in the WM class `loan-action`. Once this rule has fired, the inference engine will not have any more rules in the conflict set because it is the last rule to fire and the program will stop because no production is true. The demon in Example 3.16(b) will fire if `demon-test` and `more-data` have the most recent access tags and the delimiter is `continue`. The action in Example 3.16(b), lines 6, 7, 8, clears WM of all classes except the `loan-action`. This is done so that when the `initialize-WM` rule fires again, there will be only one instantiation of an applicant's class, of the `demon-test` class, and of the `more-delimiter` class. Example 3.16(b), line 9, will cause the `initialize-WM` rule to be placed in the conflict set again and subsequently fired.

Example 3.16. File demons

(a)

```
(p demon-check-file-stop
  {(demon-test)<dt>}
  {(more-data  ^delimiter stop) <md>}
   (loan-action ^approve <approve> ^disapprove <dapprove>)
 -->
   (closefile appdata)
   (write (crlf) |Approved Loan Applicants | <approve>)
   (write (crlf) |Disapproved Loan Applicants | <dapprove>))
```

(b)

```
(p demon-check-file-restart
  {(demon-test) <dt>}
  {(more-data  ^delimiter continue) <md>}
  {(applicant) <app>}
 -->
   (remove <dt>)
   (remove <md>)
   (remove <app>)
   (make start2))
```

If the designer wanted to save the values of the loan-action class (which are lost when the program is finished), then a file has to be opened and the values stored. This can be done by rewriting the demons in Example 3.16 (the new rules appear in Example 3.17(b), lines 6, 11, 13). Example 3.17(a), line 6, shows what would have to be changed in the initial rule to accommodate the rewritten demon (accessing a new file).

Example 3.17. Writing data to files

(a)

```
1    (p open-data-file
2        {(start)<st>}
3      -->
4        (remove <st>)
5        (openfile loanapp |RESULTS.DAT| out)
6        (openfile appdata |LQ.DAT| in)
7        (make start2)  )
```

(b)

```
1    (p demon-check-file-stop
2        {(demon-test)<dt>}
3        {(more-data  ^delimiter stop) <md>}
4      -->
5        (closefile appdata)
6        (closefile loanapp))
```

```
(p demon-check-file-restart
   {(demon-test)<dt>}
   {(more-data  ^delimiter continue) <md>}
   {(applicant)<app>}
   (loan-action ^approve <approve> ^disapprove <dapprove>)
  -->
   (write loanapp  <approve> <dapprove>)
   (remove <dt>)
   (remove <md>)
   (remove <app>)
   (make start2))
```

3.4.2 Vector Attributes

The WM elements that have been used with the LQ program so far were designed to hold only one value at a time. This is fine if the data is limited to a single value, but there are many times when a list of data is needed. For example, the data class `loan-action` can be simplified if it is implemented as lists. The `check-debt-approve` and `check-debt-disapprove` rules now instantiate new templates of the class `loan-action` for every instance of an applicant being disapproved or approved. If there were one hundred applicants, then it is possible that the WM could be loaded with one hundred instances of the class `loan-action`. If WM could contain lists within the class `loan-action`, then it would require less memory, it would be less complicated, and this list would contain a running account of all the names of the approved and disapproved applicants. In fact, OPS5 does have a list facility that allows vectors to be set up in WM. A vector is another name for list or array and there is a limit of one vector allowed per class template. Example 3.18 shows how the literalization section of the LQ program would look if the `loan-action` class was rewritten as two classes: `loan-action-disapprove` and `loan-action-approve`. Notice in Example 3.18, line 3, the new command called `vector-attribute`. This tells the WM to reserve extra space for the attributes listed as vector attributes because they will contain more than one item of data. The attributes `dlist` and `alist` have to be both literalized and vectorized if they are going to contain lists. Now the rules `check-debt-disapprove` and `check-debt-approve` have to be rewritten to access these lists.

Example 3.18. Using vector attributes

```
1    (literalize loan-action-approve alist)
2    (literalize loan-action-disapprove dlist)
3    (vector-attribute alist dlist)
```

Example 3.19 shows `check-debt-approve` accessing the vector alist. It would be easy enough to use the vectors but for one problem: There are no index variables associated with the vectors. This means that OPS5 does not provide a mechanism to keep track of where the data is in a vector. Therefore, if the code for `check-debt-approve` were run, it would constantly overwrite the first value in alist, producing a list with only one name in it: the name of the applicant that was entered when the check-debt-approve rule last fired. To make the rule in Example 3.19 work correctly, WM must be told the exact location in which to store <ntemp>. This is done by using the RHS command (litval *argument*). This procedure returns the physical WM location for the argument. This argument is temporary and must be assigned to a variable so that it can be used. The way to do this is through the bind command (the bind command was discussed in Chapter 2): (bind <vectloc> (litval alist)).

Example 3.19. Debt approval using vectors

```
(p check-debt-approve
   (applicant ^name <ntemp> ^debt-plus-halfdebt <dtemp>)
   (applicant ^halfincome-plus-savings > <dtemp>)
   { <laa> (loan-action-approve)}
-->
   (modify 1 ^loan-status tentative)
   (modify <laa> ^alist <ntemp>))
```

This line of RHS code finds the physical memory address that has been assigned to the name alist and stores that address in the variable <vectloc>. The physical address is the base location that will be used to store and retrieve data in the list. Now if the program wants to modify the vector alist, then it must use the location in <vectloc>, for example: (modify <laa> ^<vectloc> <ntemp>). Therefore, the actual name of a vector is used by OPS5 only to locate the vector in memory. All access of the vector is done through variables that are bound to the locator determined by litval. Now the check-debt-approve rule can be rewritten:

Example 3.20. Rule with bugs

```
(p check-debt-approve
   (applicant ^name <ntemp> ^debt-plus-halfdebt <dtemp>)
   (applicant ^halfincome-plus-savings > <dtemp>)
   { <laa> (loan-action-approve)}
  -->
   (modify 1 ^loan-status tentative)
   (bind <vectloc> (litval alist))
   (modify <laa> ^<vectloc> <ntemp>))
```

The code above will work but it still has a problem. Notice that the location that is bound every time is the litval of alist. This is the starting location of the vector and will always be the same location. Once again, the vector will end up with only one name in it because the first location will be continuously overwritten. An index must be used so that the rule will sequence through the vector and this index is directly related to the vector's base address (i.e., location of the first word in the vector). The definition and use of an index is the responsibility of the program designer. The following code shows how the literalization section can be changed to include the index attribute:

```
(literalize
loan-action-approve aindex alist) (literalize loan-action-disapprove
dindex dlist)

(vector-attribute alist dlist)
```

Now the RHS of the check-debt-approve rule can use the index to determine the next free location in the alist. There are two things that have to be taken into account when using an index. First, the index must be cleared initially, and second, the index must be updated after it is used.

To satisfy the first constraint, the index should be initialized with the value 0 (zero) by the RHS of the initialize-WM rule. The second constraint can be satisfied by the compute command to increment the index. Rule check-debt-approve can be rewritten using a vector index:

Example 3.21. Using a vector index

```
1   (p check-debt-approve
2      (applicant ^name <ntemp> ^debt-plus-halfdebt <dtemp>)
3      (applicant ^halfincome-plus-savings > <dtemp>)
4      {<laa> (loan-action-approve  ^aindex <adex>)}
5    -->

6      (modify 1 ^loan-status tentative)
7      (bind <vectloc> (litval alist))
8      (bind <nextloc> (compute <vectloc> + <adex>))
9      (modify <laa> ^aindex (compute <adex> + 1)
10                      ^<nextloc> <ntemp>))
```

In line 7 of this example, we find the initial location of the vector alist and bind it to the variable <vectloc>. Notice that litval uses the vector name alist without directly referencing it in the LHS. Line 8 adds the index to the initial address, which produces the next free address in the list and binds it to the variable <nextloc>. For example, if the command (litval alist) returned the number 100, then the vector alist is at memory location 100. Therefore, data can be stored at this location. And if more data is to be stored, then it must be stored sequentially starting at the initial location and incrementing upward: the second piece of data is at location 101 (vectorloc + 1), the third piece of data is at location 102 (vectorloc + 2), and so on. The index variable <adex> is used as an offset in the rule above. The index as used here will always represent how many values there are in the vector, plus one more. That means it points to the next location in the list, taken sequentially from the initial address (base address) of the list. Line 9 computes the next open location and stores it in the index attribute while line 10 stores the name of the most recently approved applicant on to the vector. This is how vectors can be used in OPS5. Example 3.22 shows how the check-debt-disapprove rule would look if it also used vectors.

Example 3.22. Rule check-debt-disapprove with vectors

```
(p check-debt-disapprove
   (applicant ^name <ntemp> ^debt <dtemp>)
   (applicant ^income < <dtemp> ^savings < <dtemp>)
   { <lad> (loan-action-disapprove  ^dindex <ddex>)}
-->
   (modify 1 ^loan-status disapproved)
   (bind <vectloc> (litval dlist))
   (bind <nextloc> (compute <vectloc> + <ddex>))
   (modify <lad>  ^dindex (compute <ddex> + 1) ^<nextloc> <ntemp>))
```

Another way of accessing values within a vector is by using the command `(substr` *vector-class begin-address end-address*`)`. This allows the designer to isolate substrings (a group of one or more values) within the vector. The variables that are called `begin-address` and `end-address` represent the bounds of the substring in the vector, and these addresses must all relate to the initial start address. For example, if the designer wanted to display the fifth name in the vector alist, the following code could be used:

Example 3.23. Isolating substrings with substr

```
        .
        .
        .
-->
  (bind <vectloc> (litval alist))
  (bind <fifthname> (compute <vectloc> + 5))
  (write (crlf) (substr <laa> <fifthname> <fifthname>))
```

If the designer wanted to store the fifth through tenth names in alist to a file, this code could be used:

Example 3.24. Writing substrings to a file

```
(p demon-check-file-stop
   {(demon-test)<dt>}
   {(more-data  ^delimiter stop) <md>}
   {<laa> (loan-action-approve)}
-->
   (closefile appdata)
   (bind <vectloc> (litval alist))
   (bind <fifthname> (compute <vectloc> + 5))
   (bind <tenthname> (compute <vectloc> +10))
   (openfile loanapp |RESULTS.DAT| out)
   (write loanapp  (substr <laa> <fifthname> <tenthname>))
   (closefile loanapp))
```

Finally, if the designer wanted to store both the approved list and the disapproved list in files, then the code in Example 3.25 could be used. Notice that in lines 11 and 14, the last argument in the `substr` commands is `inf`. This is a special `substr` keyword and it tells the `substr` function to get all the values from the location designated by the first argument, up to the last value that has been stored in the vector.

Example 3.25. Use of substr with inf

```
1  (p demon-check-file-stop
2        {(demon-test)<dt>}
3        {(more-data  ^delimiter stop) <md>}
4        {<laa> (loan-action-approve ^aindex <adex>)}
5        {<lad> (loan-action-disapprove ^dindex <ddex>)}
6     -->
7        (closefile appdata)
8        (bind <avectloc> (litval alist))
9        (bind <dvectloc> (litval dlist))
10       (openfile loanapp |RESAPP.DAT| out)
11       (write loanapp  (substr <laa> <avectloc>  inf))
12       (closefile loanapp)
13       (openfile loandisapp |RESDIS.DAT| out)
14       (write loandisapp  (substr <lad> <dvectloc>  inf))
15       (closefile loandisapp))
```

This is the way OPS5 allows the user to develop lists. The indexes are essentially pointers that can move forward and backward through the list and the designer can have as many pointers as needed. The minimum number of pointers needed for a vector to work properly is one. The `substr` command allows the designer to break vectors up into smaller units and is useful if the lists contain modules. The number of values that can be contained in a vector varies between implementations of OPS5 and the designer is advised to check the user's manual for the exact number of values that can be stored per vector so that there is no possibility of overflow. Also note that the values can be text or numbers.

OPS5 vectors are powerful because the user can structure them in different ways. The use of pointers and indexes allow the designer to implement more complex structures, such as linked lists, queues, and stacks.

3.5 SUMMARY

This chapter covered the concept of controlling an OPS5 program through the wise use of rules. The difference between the MEA and LEX conflict resolution strategies was discussed. The concept of demons was introduced, as well as arithmetic operations, file I/O, and arrays. In the next chapter, we will investigate how to apply standard programming techniques to the OPS5 language.

3.6 PROBLEMS

1. What should be performed in the first rule that fires in an OPS5 program? How can you be sure that a specific rule will fire first? Explain your answer.
2. Write a rule that will be the first to fire in a program that has the following literalized WM and show what you have to do to get the rule to fire:

```
(literalize auto make model color)
(literalize first)
```

3. Why would a program use the **remove** command? Explain how it relates to "access tags".
4. When would you use the **modify** command, and when would you use the **make** command? How does each affect WM and the access tags?
5. Show how LEX and MEA would resolve the conflict of the following rules:

```
              Time            Time             Time
              Tags            Tags             Tags

(a) Rule1: 1         Rule2: 9         Rule3: 3
           5                1                2
           2                                 8

(b) Rule1: 9         Rule2: 2         Rule3: 3
           3                4                9
          10                3                1

(c) Rule1: 7         Rule2: 1         Rule3: 1
           5                7                2
           9                6
```

6. Explain how LEX helps to control the flow of rules in an OPS5 program. Write three small rules that continue the program started in Problem 2. Make these rules fire in order by using the following routing variable:

```
(literalize rout rule_number)
```

7. Write a small program (three rules) that will input a value as Fahrenheit or Celsius, perform the conversion to the opposite temperature, and then print the results. As a reminder, the following formulas may be used:

```
F=(9/5 * C) + 32            C = (F - 32) * 5/9
```

8. Rewrite the rule in problem 7 so that it inputs values from a file.
9. Add a rule to the program written in problem 7 that will store the temperature conversions in a file.
10. Rewrite the literalization section so that the class **auto** is represented by a vector attribute instead of individual attributes.

4

PROGRAMMING TECHNIQUES

4.1 ITERATION AND RECURSION

Iteration and recursion are important control concepts in programming. Iteration is common in any language: BASIC, C, and Pascal all have `FOR` loops and Common LISP has a very general `DO` loop. Even in assembly language, programmers quickly learn how to do iteration. Iteration allows us to perform an operation a number of times, or perhaps on a number of objects. Not only does iteration allow us to be more concise, but it allows us to be more general. Consider the following Pascal code for printing five carriage returns:

```
writeln();
writeln();
writeln();
writeln();
writeln();
```

Any novice Pascal programmer could quickly convert that to

```
for i := 1 to 5 do
   writeln();
```

A programmer who had a bit more experience would want to generalize the loop in order to handle any number of carriage returns, and might produce the following procedure:

```
procedure cr(n : integer);
begin
var
   i : integer;

   for i := 1 to n do
      writeln();
end;
```

Of course, there will be times where we would like to perform iteration in OPS5. We may want to do something a certain number of times, or we may want to perform the same operation on a number of objects. Remember that in OPS5, we must express ourselves just with rules and their interactions with working memory (WM). It turns out that some kinds of iteration require a bit of work in OPS5, and some kinds come "for free," in the sense that they happen automatically (which in some cases might be undesirable).

Suppose you have an array of numbers that you would like to print out, and you that you do not care much about the order. First, we will do it in Pascal:

```
program print();
var
  nums : array[1..10] of int;
  i : int;
begin
  nums[1] = 72;
  (* initialize num[2] to num[10] here in the same way *)

  for i := 1 to 10 do
     writeln(i, ' = ', nums[i]);
end.
```

In OPS5, a similar thing would be even easier. Suppose we had defined a working memory type as follows:

```
(literalize nums index value)
```

We would then initialize these variables in working memory with `make` commands, such as this: `(make nums ^index 1 ^value 72)`, which would put the value `72` in "location" `1`. This is not a real array in the way that Pascal or C would store it, but simply part of working memory that we are using to mimic an array. The actual order in which the working memory elements are stored depends on the order in which they are created. In order to print out all the values, we could use the following OPS5 rule and let it run until all members of the conflict set have been fired:

```
(p print-values
   (num ^index <i> ^value <v>)
```

```
-->
   (write (crlf) <i> | = | <v>))
```

You may be surprised at the order in which the values are printed. Remember how conflict resolution works. It looks at all instantiations (rules and their matching data) in the conflict set, and in the case of ties, the more recent working memory elements win. So `print-values` will fire for every working memory element (WME) of type `num` that it sees, but they will be printed in the reverse order in which they were created. If you are printing out values, the order often does matter, but there are many other operations where order does not matter and you can use this easy method of iteration.

A second type of iteration requires us to create and maintain our own loop counters in working memory. This type of iteration will be very much like the type available in Pascal or C. Suppose the literalizations are as before, with one addition:

```
(literalize nums index value)
(literalize current-counter val)
```

We could then have a rule that was only a bit more complex then the preceding rule:

```
(p print-values-in-order
   (current-counter ^val <i>)
   (nums ^index <i> ^value <v>)
-->
   (write (crlf) <i> | = | <v>)
   (modify 1 ^val (compute <i> + 1)))
```

As before, we create our data in working memory with things of the form `(make nums ^index 1 ^value 72)`, but we must also initialize the loop counter as follows: `(make current-counter ^val 1)`. Assuming that the index values are 1 through 10, this will print all values in numerical order.

So far, we have learned how to iterate where we do not care about the order that things happen in, and we have learned how to iterate when the objects we are interested in are neatly numbered with consecutive digits. What about the case where things are not so perfect? Suppose we have an array of numbers, and we would like to print out only those array locations with values between 10 and 20. At first, it may seem like a simple modification to the previous rule as follows:

```
(p broken-print-values-in-range-in-order
   (current-counter ^val <i>)
   (nums ^index <i> ^value <v> > 10 < 20)
-->
   (write (crlf) <i> | = | <v>)
   (modify 1 ^val (compute <i> + 1)))
```

But as soon as we encounter a value that is not between 10 and 20, this rule will not fire, and our current-counter will not be incremented. We can solve this problem in the following way:

```
(p print-values-in-range-in-order
   (current-counter ^val <i>)
   (nums ^index <j> > <i> ^value {<v1> > 10 < 20})
  -(nums ^index {< <j> > <i>} ^value > 10 < 20)
-->
   (write (crlf) <i> | = | <v>)
   (modify 1 ^val <j>))
```

The first pattern on the left-hand side obviously matches the current counter and binds its value to <i>. The second pattern would match any number with index greater than the current counter with a value in the proper range. The third pattern, however, guarantees that there is no number in the proper range that has a lower index than the one in the second pattern. Note that no variables are allowed to be bound in a negated pattern, since they could not be bound to a pattern that does not exist. The first action simply writes out the matching number, and the second action bumps up current-counter to the index of the number that just matched. A technique like this would also be useful for a *sparse array*, in which there are values stored only for a small fraction of the possible indexes. In a language like C or Pascal, you would have to do a good deal of work to store and access such an array efficiently. In OPS5, there is no such thing as an empty working memory element, so you would be using only as many places as you need.

Recursion is a powerful concept and is used quite often by proficient Pascal, C, and LISP programmers. This book is not the place to learn what recursion is, but if you are already familiar with recursion in another programming language, it will not be difficult to understand recursion in OPS5. Think for a minute about what recursion is: It is a divide-and-conquer technique, where one applies the same methods to smaller and smaller pieces of the data until the problem is reduced to a trivial one. The classic (and in some ways the simplest) recursion example is calculating the factorial of a number. Many computer language texts include factorials as an example of recursion. We would not want to disappoint you, so here goes: Remember that $n! = (n)\underbrace{(n-1)(n-2)\ldots(2)(1)}_{(n-1)!}$.
So, we could implement factorial recursively as n times $(n-1)!$, where 1! is defined to be 1.

Let's create a working memory type to represent the factorials:

```
(literalize factorial number result)
```

Now, we will need a few rules to do the actual calculations.

```
; factorial of n - 1 is not known. try to compute it
(p make-recursive-goal
```

```
   (factorial ^number <n> > 1 ^result nil)
  -(factorial ^number = <n> - 1)
-->
   (make factorial ^number (compute <n> - 1)))

; if we need the factorial of 1, return a 1
(p calculate-factorial-1
   (factorial ^number 1 ^result nil)
-->
   (modify 1 ^result 1))

; if we know the factorial of n - 1 but not n, compute it
(p perform-multiply
   (factorial ^number <n1> ^result nil)
   (factorial ^number = <n1> - 1 ^result <r> <> nil)
-->
   (modify 1 ^result (compute <n1> * <r>)))
```

We can make the program calculate the factorial of 5 by typing `(make factorial ^number 5 ^result nil)` and `(run)`. If we run this program for a number n, the factorials for all integers between n and 1 will be left in working memory when the rules finish firing. If you will be computing more factorials later, they will be computed even faster, since you already have a table of some factorials available. If computing a factorial is a one-time event in some larger program, you may want to clean working memory up after the factorial calculation. This can be done by adding a `(remove 2)` to the RHS of `perform-multiply`. This cleans up the extra intermediate `factorial` working memory elements as soon as they are used.

In this example of recursion, we started at n, and wound our way down to 1. When we found the result for 1, we unwound our way back out to n. In OPS5, as in every other language, there is more than one way to do everything. As an exercise, you may want to write a version that starts at 1 and works its way up to n. Also, it is easy to write an iterative version of `factorial` that does not create intermediate working memory elements. This would be useful when calculating factorials where n is huge.

4.2 PARTITIONING RULE SETS

One obvious difference between OPS5 and other programming languages is that OPS5 has a very flat hierarchy in terms of control and data structures. What do we mean by hierarchy? In languages such as C, one typically breaks a program down into modules and functions. Once a certain function is debugged, it can be thought of as a "black box" in the programmer's mind. If a function is truly debugged, its internals need not be considered when debugging another part of the program. This tremendously reduces complexity and aids program understanding. In OPS5, there is no built-in mechanism for reducing complexity. When debugging a 1000-rule system that was poorly designed, the programmer might have to think about any of the rules at any given time.

As a technique for reducing complexity, one can carefully structure a large rule base so that only a fraction of the rules need to be considered at any time. Knowledge can be partitioned. This is natural, because most tasks can be broken into independent subproblems. This makes some sense intuitively: Humans think very little about how to mix orange juice when they are diagnosing clutches. OPS5 handles large rule bases efficiently in the matching process, but conflict resolution can only take longer with a large conflict set.

Fortunately, it is quite easy in OPS5 to partition a rule set, as long as you can nicely divide the problem. By adding a new type of working memory element to the LHS of every rule, we can control which sets of rules can fire at any time. Let's literalize the new type:

```
(literalize focus is)
```

Now, let's write some rules where the first pattern looks like this:

```
(p orange-juice-rule-1
   (focus ^is orange-juice)
 .
 .
 .
-->
 .
 .
 .
)
```

And some others where the first pattern looks like this:

```
(p diagnose-clutch-rule-1
   (focus ^is clutch)
 .
 .
 .
-->
 .
 .
 .
)
```

If we do a `(make focus ^is orange-juice)`, then obviously only the first kind of rule can fire. If we later do a `modify` that changes the `focus` to `clutch`, then only the second type of rule can fire. There has to be an orange juice rule (with `focus ^is orange-juice)`) that contains this modify. You can either add that to an existing orange juice rule, or add a new one that looks like this:

```
(p change-focus
   (focus ^is orange-juice)
-->
   (modify 1 ^is clutch))
```

You need not worry about this rule firing too soon. The conflict resolution strategies favor more complex rules over simpler ones, so a rule this simple will always be the last to fire in the orange juice context.

4.3 POWERFUL ONE-RULE PROGRAMS

The programming language APL is very powerful, yet it can be very difficult for people to read APL code. Computer scientists delight in composing obscure "one-line" APL programs, and then challenging their colleagues to decipher what the program does. OPS5 contains a powerful pattern matcher, and you can do surprising things with just one rule. In this section we show examples of interesting one-rule systems. OPS5 is a fairly readable language, and with some practice, you will be able to look at OPS5 rules and quickly understand what they do.

4.3.1 Massive Comparisons

The first example is quite similar to a database query. In some ways, working memory in OPS5 is like a relational database. If you consider each record from a database to be a working memory element in OPS5, you can see the connection. Suppose we have a working memory type called **person**, which has fields for `name` and `savings`:

```
(literalize person name savings)
```

Suppose we are poor starving graduate students, and we would like to invite the wealthiest of our friends out for dinner (in the hopes that they will pick up the tab). In OPS5's pattern-matching paradigm, we can phrase this as: *Find the person such that no other person has greater savings.* That can be written as the following OPS5 rule:

```
(p find-wealthiest-person
   (person ^name <name> ^savings <s>)
  -(person ^savings { > <s> } )
-->
   (write (crlf) <name> is the wealthiest person (crlf)))
```

Now, let's add the working memory elements for the persons. Remember that no working memory elements can be made until the last rule has been read in. (See Chapter 6 to understand the reasons for this.)

```
(make person ^name al ^savings 30000)
(make person ^name bob ^savings 2000)
(make person ^name cathy ^savings 100)
(make person ^name dave ^savings 100000)
(make person ^name elaine ^savings 5000)
(make person ^name frank ^savings 20)
(make person ^name gary ^savings 0)
(make person ^name heidi ^savings 700)
```

Let's run the system and see the results.

```
> (load "wealth.ops")

> (wm)
1:  (PERSON   ^NAME AL     ^SAVINGS 30000)
2:  (PERSON   ^NAME BOB     ^SAVINGS 2000)
3:  (PERSON   ^NAME CATHY     ^SAVINGS 100)
4:  (PERSON   ^NAME DAVE    ^SAVINGS 100000)
5:  (PERSON   ^NAME ELAINE     ^SAVINGS 5000)
6:  (PERSON   ^NAME FRANK     ^SAVINGS 20)
7:  (PERSON   ^NAME GARY    ^SAVINGS 0)
8:  (PERSON   ^NAME HEIDI     ^SAVINGS 700)
NIL

> (cs)
FIND-WEALTHIEST-PERSON
(FIND-WEALTHIEST-PERSON DOMINATES)
```

When we type (wm), we see the eight people represented in working memory. We also see that one rule in the system is ready to fire when we examine the conflict set. We then run the system:

```
> (run)

1. FIND-WEALTHIEST-PERSON 4
DAVE IS THE WEALTHIEST PERSON

end -- no production true
  1 productions (5 // 6 nodes)
  1 firings (8 rhs actions)
  8 mean working memory size (8 maximum)
  1 mean conflict set size (1 maximum)
 16 mean token memory size (16 maximum)
NIL
> (quit)
```

This tells us that Dave is the wealthiest person, so we invite him to dinner!

4.3.2 Traveling Salesman Problem

The second example in this section is the traveling salesman problem, which is a classic problem in Computer Science. Given a set of cities that must be visited, we would like to find the shortest path that visits each city exactly once. For a small number of cities, it is reasonable to find the best tour by looking at all possible paths. As the number of cities grows, this quickly becomes out of the question because of the time needed to look at all the tours. For five cities, the number of unique tours is 5 factorial or 120, while for 10 cities, it would be 10 factorial or more than 3,600,000. For more than 10 cities, it quickly climbs beyond hope of solution by exhaustive search. Fortunately, there are some techniques that do a reasonable job without looking at all possible paths. One of them is called the *nearest neighbor* technique, because it involves picking a city that has not been completely connected, and connecting it to the nearest neighboring city that has not been completely connected. There are many problems that can be thought of in the same way as the traveling salesman problem. Suppose you were in charge of installing a computer network among 50 personal computers in your building. A good layout which minimizes the total amount of cable could save hundreds of dollars and hours of climbing up through ceilings. By thinking of each office as a city, you can use the traveling salesman code to find the best way to connect the computers.

Let's build a working memory element, called **city**, that will contain a name and a number represening the number of connections to other cities.

```
(literalize city name connections)
```

We also need to represent the paths between cities, so we will literalize a class called path which has two cities as fields, a place for the distance between the cities, and a flag to show whether the path has been chosen.

```
(literalize path city1 city2 distance chosen)
```

We now create a rule which looks at all the paths that involve not completely connected cities, and picks the shortest one.

```
(p grab-shortest-path
     {(city ^name <a> ^connections {<c1> < 2}) <city1>}
     {(city ^name {<b> <> <a>} ^connections {<c2> < 2}) <city2>}
     {(path ^city1 <a> ^city2 <b> ^distance <v> ^chosen nil) <dist1>}
     {(path ^city1 <b> ^city2 <a> ^distance <v> ^chosen nil) <dist2>}
    -(path ^city1 <x> ^city2 <y> ^distance { < <v>} ^chosen nil)
-->
     (write (crlf) |The closest cities are | <a> | and | <b> (crlf))
     (write (crlf) |distance is | <v> (crlf))
     (modify <dist1> ^chosen yes)
     (modify <dist2> ^chosen yes)
     (modify <city1> ^connections (compute <c1> + 1))
     (modify <city2> ^connections (compute <c2> + 1)))
```

We must put our cities in working memory, and that is done with a **make** for each city:

```
(make city ^name new-york ^connections 0)
(make city ^name miami ^connections 0)
(make city ^name austin ^connections 0)
(make city ^name chicago ^connections 0)
(make city ^name los-angeles ^connections 0)
```

We must also create working memory elements to represent the distances.

```
(make path ^city1 new-york ^city2 miami       ^distance 80)
(make path ^city1 new-york ^city2 austin      ^distance 89)
(make path ^city1 new-york ^city2 chicago     ^distance 41)
(make path ^city1 new-york ^city2 los-angeles ^distance 108)

(make path ^city1 miami    ^city2 new-york    ^distance 80)
(make path ^city1 miami    ^city2 austin      ^distance 40)
(make path ^city1 miami    ^city2 chicago     ^distance 80)
(make path ^city1 miami    ^city2 los-angeles ^distance 92)

(make path ^city1 austin   ^city2 new-york    ^distance 89)
(make path ^city1 austin   ^city2 miami       ^distance 40)
(make path ^city1 austin   ^city2 chicago     ^distance 70)
(make path ^city1 austin   ^city2 los-angeles ^distance 53)

(make path ^city1 chicago   ^city2 new-york    ^distance 41)
(make path ^city1 chicago   ^city2 miami       ^distance 80)
(make path ^city1 chicago   ^city2 austin      ^distance 70)
(make path ^city1 chicago   ^city2 los-angeles ^distance 70)

(make path ^city1 los-angeles  ^city2 new-york  ^distance 108)
(make path ^city1 los-angeles  ^city2 miami     ^distance 92)
(make path ^city1 los-angeles  ^city2 austin    ^distance 53)
(make path ^city1 los-angeles  ^city2 chicago   ^distance 70)
```

Now, we run the system, and watch the cities get connected.

```
> (run)
1. GRAB-SHORTEST-PATH 3 2 15 11
The closest cities are  AUSTIN  and  MIAMI

distance is  40

2. GRAB-SHORTEST-PATH 1 4 8 18
The closest cities are  NEW-YORK  and  CHICAGO

distance is  41

3. GRAB-SHORTEST-PATH 31 5 17 24
The closest cities are  AUSTIN  and  LOS-ANGELES

distance is  53

4. GRAB-SHORTEST-PATH 41 49 21 25
The closest cities are  CHICAGO  and  LOS-ANGELES
```

```
distance is  70

end -- no production true
 1 PRODUCTIONS (14 // 23 NODES)
 4 FIRINGS (57 RHS ACTIONS)
 25 MEAN WORKING MEMORY SIZE (25 MAXIMUM)
 2 MEAN CONFLICT SET SIZE (2 MAXIMUM)
 72 MEAN TOKEN MEMORY SIZE (85 MAXIMUM)
NIL
```

4.3.3 Bubble Sort

Many sorting algorithms exist. The best one for a given job is dependent on things such as the number of items to be sorted, the amount of memory available, and the amount of programming effort that you want to expend. If you are writing a sort routine that is seldom used, you might as well select a slower but easy-to-program algorithm. On the other hand, an often-used sort routine included with an operating system should be as fast as possible. One characteristic of sorting algorithms in Pascal or C is that the faster they are, the more unreadable the code seems to be. Some sorting methods are rather intuitive and the code is trivial to read; other methods require a bit of study to capture the subtleties. In this section, we will present a very intuitive method for sorting an array of numbers. It may not be the most efficient sorting algorithm, but it is easy to program, easy to understand, and elegantly shows the power of OPS5.

The most used sorts tend to have interesting names: Shell Sort, Quicksort, Insertion Sort, and so on. We will implement Bubble Sort in OPS5, which takes its name from the fact that smaller values "bubble" to the top of the array. It is so simple that we will first present the code and then comment on it.

```
(literalize element position value)

; if there are two elements such that the value of the lower numbered
; one is higher than the higher numbered one, swap their values
(p bubble-sort
  {(element ^position <p1> ^value <v1>) <first>}
  {(element ^position {<p2> > <p1>} ^value {<v2> < <v1>}) <second>}
-->
  (modify <first> ^value <v2>)
  (modify <second> ^value <v1>))

(make element ^position 1 ^value 43)
(make element ^position 2 ^value 13)
(make element ^position 3 ^value 97)
(make element ^position 4 ^value 4)
(make element ^position 5 ^value 22)
(make element ^position 6 ^value 120)
(make element ^position 7 ^value 56)
(make element ^position 8 ^value 0)
```

The rule `bubble-sort` simply says that if there is an element in a position with a certain value, and an element in a higher position with a lower value, then swap their values. The array in working memory is initialized by calling `make` for each element.

We load in the code for the Bubble Sort, examine working memory, then run the system:

```
> (load "bubble.ops")
;;; Loading source file "bubble.ops"
*

> (wm)

1:  (ELEMENT    ^POSITION 1     ^VALUE 43)
2:  (ELEMENT    ^POSITION 2     ^VALUE 13)
3:  (ELEMENT    ^POSITION 3     ^VALUE 97)
4:  (ELEMENT    ^POSITION 4     ^VALUE 4)
5:  (ELEMENT    ^POSITION 5     ^VALUE 22)
6:  (ELEMENT    ^POSITION 6     ^VALUE 120)
7:  (ELEMENT    ^POSITION 7     ^VALUE 56)
8:  (ELEMENT    ^POSITION 8     ^VALUE 0)
NIL

> (cs)
BUBBLE-SORT     (15 occurrences)
(BUBBLE-SORT DOMINATES)

> (run)
1. BUBBLE-SORT 7 8
2. BUBBLE-SORT 6 12
3. BUBBLE-SORT 14 10
4. BUBBLE-SORT 3 20
5. BUBBLE-SORT 22 18
6. BUBBLE-SORT 2 26
7. BUBBLE-SORT 32 4
8. BUBBLE-SORT 1 36
9. BUBBLE-SORT 40 5
10. BUBBLE-SORT 38 34
11. BUBBLE-SORT 46 30
end -- no production true
  1 productions (4 // 6 nodes)
 11 firings (52 rhs actions)
  8 mean working memory size (8 maximum)
  8 mean conflict set size (15 maximum)
  8 mean token memory size (8 maximum)
NIL
```

We now examine working memory and see that the values have switched position in the array, and are now sorted. The order in which the working memory elements are printed out depends on the recency of their time tags, so they are almost but not exactly in reverse position order.

```
> (wm)
16:  (ELEMENT    ^POSITION 8    ^VALUE 120)
24:  (ELEMENT    ^POSITION 7    ^VALUE 97)
28:  (ELEMENT    ^POSITION 6    ^VALUE 56)
42:  (ELEMENT    ^POSITION 4    ^VALUE 22)
44:  (ELEMENT    ^POSITION 5    ^VALUE 43)
48:  (ELEMENT    ^POSITION 3    ^VALUE 13)
50:  (ELEMENT    ^POSITION 1    ^VALUE 0)
52:  (ELEMENT    ^POSITION 2    ^VALUE 4)
NIL
> (quit)
```

4.3.4 Population Densities

The next example is actually a two-rule system, but one rule simply serves to make things more convenient, and the second rule does the complex pattern matching. First, we literalize a working memory element type for `city` that includes a name, area, population, and density. We assume that only the area and population need to be entered initially, and the first rule will fire and fill in the computed density for each city. The second rule says, in effect: *If there is a city such that no city has a lower density, and there is also a city such that no city has a higher density, print out the names of these two cities.* There is also a pattern that makes sure that all city densities have been filled in. This assures that the second rule does not fire until the first is completely finished.

```
(literalize city name area population density)

(p calculate-densities
   {(city ^name <n1> ^area <area1> ^population <p1> ^density nil) <city>}
-->
    (modify <city> ^density (compute <p1> // <area1>)))

(p find-densest-and-sparsest-city
   (city ^name <empty-city> ^density <d1>)
  -(city ^density <d2> < <d1>)
   (city ^name <crowded-city> ^density <d3>)
  -(city ^density <d4> > <d3>)
  -(city ^density nil)
-->
   (write (crlf) |The densest city is | <crowded-city>
           | and the least crowded is | <empty-city> (crlf)))

(make city ^name boca-raton ^area 121 ^population 10000)
(make city ^name key-largo  ^area 87  ^population 500)
(make city ^name cromwell   ^area 21  ^population 7000)
```

```
(make city ^name deerfield  ^area 414 ^population 4500)
(make city ^name lantana    ^area 67  ^population 6700)
(make city ^name harrison   ^area 203 ^population 1500)
(make city ^name scarsdale  ^area 324 ^population 640)
```

We load in the file, and examine working memory. The conflict set contains seven instantiations of `calculate-densities`, one for each city.

```
> load "pop.ops")
> ;;; Loading source file "pop.ops"
**

> (wm)
1:  (CITY   ^NAME BOCA-RATON   ^AREA 121   ^POPULATION 10000)
2:  (CITY   ^NAME KEY-LARGO   ^AREA 87   ^POPULATION 500)
3:  (CITY   ^NAME CROMWELL   ^AREA 21   ^POPULATION 7000)
4:  (CITY   ^NAME DEERFIELD   ^AREA 414   ^POPULATION 4500)
5:  (CITY   ^NAME LANTANA   ^AREA 67   ^POPULATION 6700)
6:  (CITY   ^NAME HARRISON   ^AREA 203   ^POPULATION 1500)
7:  (CITY   ^NAME SCARSDALE   ^AREA 324   ^POPULATION 640)
NIL

> (cs)
CALCULATE-DENSITIES     (7 occurrences)
(CALCULATE-DENSITIES DOMINATES)

> (run 7)
1. CALCULATE-DENSITIES 7
2. CALCULATE-DENSITIES 6
3. CALCULATE-DENSITIES 5
4. CALCULATE-DENSITIES 4
5. CALCULATE-DENSITIES 3
6. CALCULATE-DENSITIES 2
7. CALCULATE-DENSITIES 1
***BREAK***
```

After running the interpreter for seven cycles, we examine working memory and see the densities all filled in. We then run the interpreter, and in one cycle it tells us the densest and least dense cities:

```
> (wm)
9:  (CITY   ^NAME SCARSDALE   ^AREA 324   ^POPULATION 640   ^DENSITY 1)
11:  (CITY   ^NAME HARRISON   ^AREA 203   ^POPULATION 1500   ^DENSITY 7)
13:  (CITY   ^NAME LANTANA   ^AREA 67   ^POPULATION 6700   ^DENSITY 100)
15:  (CITY   ^NAME DEERFIELD   ^AREA 414   ^POPULATION 4500   ^DENSITY 10)
17:  (CITY   ^NAME CROMWELL   ^AREA 21   ^POPULATION 7000   ^DENSITY 333)
19:  (CITY   ^NAME KEY-LARGO   ^AREA 87   ^POPULATION 500   ^DENSITY 5)
21:  (CITY   ^NAME BOCA-RATON   ^AREA 121   ^POPULATION 10000   ^DENSITY 82)
```

```
NIL

> (cs)
FIND-DENSEST-AND-SPARSEST-CITY
(FIND-DENSEST-AND-SPARSEST-CITY DOMINATES)

> (run)
8. FIND-DENSEST-AND-SPARSEST-CITY 9 17
The densest city is  CROMWELL  and the least crowded is  SCARSDALE

end -- no production true
  2 productions (14 // 22 nodes)
  8 firings (21 rhs actions)
  7 mean working memory size (7 maximum)
  4 mean conflict set size (7 maximum)
 76 mean token memory size (126 maximum)
NIL
> (quit)
```

4.4 SUMMARY

In this chapter we showed that OPS5 is capable of simulating standard programming techniques such as iteration and recursion. The concept of partitioning a set of rules into modules was explained, and examples were shown demonstrating these concepts. We also showed examples of how a one-rule program can do things that would require much more code in other languages. In the next chapter, we will look at a larger problem and see how it is implemented in OPS5.

4.5 PROBLEMS

1. Write two OPS5 programs that will open a file and input every other element stored in the file. The file has 100 elements in it and the last element in the file is the word `stop`. One program should demonstrate a recursive approach, and the other program should demonstrate iteration.
2. Write an OPS5 program to perform a Quicksort.

5

AN EXAMPLE PROGRAM

5.1 PROBLEM DESCRIPTION

One experience that most people have sooner or later is applying for credit, whether it be a car loan, a mortgage, or a credit card. Lenders use various rules of thumb to decide how much money to lend, and at what interest rate. Certain credit cards simply allow fixed limits, which are increased periodically if payment history is satisfactory. For example, a student might start off with a $250 limit on a credit card, and after she has paid back on time for a year, the limit might be increased to $500. Other lenders have no fixed limit, but instead decide with each charge if the borrower will exceed her ability to pay back on time. Many of the factors that go into a decision such as this can be expressed naturally as rules. For example:

- If this is the first month the card is in use, do not allow a balance of more than $1000 because most fraud occurs with new cards.
- If the customer has a perfect payment record for at least two years, allow a balance up to three times the customer's monthly take-home pay; otherwise, allow a balance of only two months' take-home pay.
- If charges totaling more than one month's pay are made in less than 48 hours, the card may be stolen, and we should call the card holder to verify the charges.

It is certainly possible to develop a very complicated formula that incorporates all of this, but that kind of formula would be extremely difficult to understand and to modify when policies change. Suppose the credit company realized that certain types of business travelers are likely to charge many times their base salary each month, yet are quite prompt at paying their bills. It would be wise to use this information when giving consideration to their credit, but it would be difficult to encode in a formula. You can see that it may be beneficial to encode this knowledge in a more lucid and flexible way so that it can be understood by newcomers, and modified as the need arises.

Rule-based systems are one good way to categorize things such as credit applications. When issuing credit, a large amount of money is often at stake, and a bank will benefit by using consistent guidelines for all borrowers, and also by being quickly able to update those guidelines as market conditions change. There may be hundreds of loan officers in a large bank, and it is desirable to have them all perform as well as the most experienced of them. It is also useful to have a system that reduces the likelihood of an oversight or error. In addition, it could be fruitful for a bank to have a system that serves as a training tool for new and less experienced employees.

We will build a prototype of such a system in OPS5, and you will see the steps required in building a small expert system. While we use some fictional numbers in this system, we have purposefully chosen a domain that would be a profitable one for applying expert systems. In fact, several very large companies in the United States use rule-based expert systems very similar to this one for making credit decisions.

There are two important things to think about when designing a program of any kind: control and data structures. Both of these will usually go through refinements during the debugging of the program, but it is usually quite valuable to spend time thinking about these things before any coding begins. In this example, we will first design the data structures, and then think about control. In the example, we will introduce new information about the domain in *italics like this*, and show OPS5 code in `bold typeface like this`.

5.2 DECLARING WORKING MEMORY

Imagine that you have been hired as a consultant to a bank to develop an interactive system for judging loan applications. The bank has given you access to one of their best loan officers, Maureen, for a few days so that you can find out about the mortgage approval process. You ask her for a brief outline of what she does, and she tells you:

> All applications are mailed to this office with some standard information about the applicants: names, addresses for the past five years, phone numbers, employers, salaries, number of dependents, and so forth. There is also information about the property that is being purchased: address, age, purchase price, and so on. Much of the evaluation process is determining what additional information is required, and then requesting it from whoever has it. It doesn't make sense to require all possible information from every applicant. When all of the necessary information is brought together, a final decision is made. For example, we don't require termite inspections in certain regions of the country, so termite reports are only requested later when necessary rather than at application time. Another example is that

we do not need to verify dividend income unless it represents more than 10 percent of the applicant's annual gross income. But I'm getting way ahead of myself here.

You would like to establish what kinds of working memory elements (WME) are required for this system. So far, it sounds like there should be a WME for an applicant, with attributes such as name, address, and salary. We can add more attributes later as we need them. We will also need a WME for the property being purchased, with attributes for price, age, and region of the country. There should also be a WME for the loan, which holds values such as loan status. Remember that an OPS5 program must declare all working memory types and attributes using a `literalize` before any rules are read in. Therefore, we have

```
(literalize applicant name address income stocks dividends savings)
(literalize property price age region appraised-value)
(literalize loan status)
```

As it turns out, we are going to need other working memory element types and attributes. If you were developing this system from scratch, you would probably add these things to the literalization section incrementally as you wrote new rules. For clarity, we will show the final literalization section now. This will allow you to type the code in this chapter in the order that it appears, and the system will work at every step of the way.

```
(literalize applicant name address income stocks dividends savings
            currentjob credit one-third-income one-sixth-income
            payment-ability)

(literalize property price age region appraised-value waste
            five-percent ten-percent twenty-percent eighty
            ninety-five one-twenty money-down
            home-value)

(literalize loan downpayment status)

(literalize phase name) ; can be one of application, info collection
                        ; categorization, evaluation, or security

(literalize economy region maxprice prices)
```

Let's focus our attention for a moment on the control in this expert system. We ask the mortgage officer what the phases of mortgage approval are. Maureen says:

The first step is to verify that all the information given to us on the application is correct and complete. After that, we decide what other information will be required, and then collect that information. Then, we categorize the quality of the downpayment, the quality of the property, and the quality of the applicant's ability to pay. We assign a value of poor, fair, good, or excellent to each of those three areas. The next phase is evaluation, and there we look at the three areas and decide whether or not to loan the money. If any area is given a poor, the loan is rejected. If any area is given an excellent and there are no poor ratings, then the loan is accepted. Otherwise, we need at least two ratings of good. Finally, the last phase assures the security of the loan, by requesting the proper insurances on the property and on the applicants, as well as certain appraisals and inspections.

So, from what the loan officer has told us, we see that control breaks down naturally into five phases. Let's call them *application*, *information collection*, *categorization*, *evaluation*, and *security*. Let's create a working memory element that will hold the phase, or context. This will allow us to limit the number of rules that can be in the conflict set at any time. This is a common technique in OPS5 programs and was discussed previously. By then putting a pattern on the left-hand side of each rule, one can essentially "partition" the rule set. This will become clearer when we write the rules. For now, let's continue by literalizing the phase:

```
(literalize phase name) ; can be one of application, info collection,
                        ; categorization, evaluation, or security
```

When we begin running the program, we will want to make a number of working memory elements. We want to create a new loan working memory element, and set the phase of the program to application. We also initialize some data on regions of the country:

```
(p initialize-things
    (start 1)
    -->
    (remove 1)
    (make loan ^status undecided)
    (make phase ^name application)
    (make economy ^region south     ^maxprice 250000 ^prices steady)
    (make economy ^region midwest   ^maxprice 125000 ^prices rising)
    (make economy ^region northeast ^maxprice 350000 ^prices falling)
    (make economy ^region west      ^maxprice 300000 ^prices rising)
)
```

We must be careful to have only one working memory element of type `phase` in working memory at any given time, or else sets of rules may be enabled at the wrong times.

5.3 ADDING SOME RULES

Those rules that will be applicable only during the application phase will all have the pattern `(phase ^name application)` in their left-hand sides. That way, only those rules can fire, and we are assured that things happen in the correct sequence. We will also need rules that cause the transition from one phase to the next, and those will look something like this:

```
; change phase from application to collection. Since it has a
; very simple left hand side, this rule will only fire if no
; other rule is in the conflict set
(p change-phase-to-collection
   {(phase ^name application) <ph>}
-->
   (write (crlf) |Moving to collection phase| (crlf))
   (modify <ph> ^name collection))
```

There will be one such rule for each of the four phase transitions. Let's go ahead and write some rules for the application phase. First, we will want to create a rule that asks for information about the applicant if none exists:

```
; if we are in the application phase, and we don't have an applicant
; in working memory, let's make one.

(p get-applicant-info
   (phase ^name application)
  -(applicant)
-->
   (write (crlf) |What is the applicant's name?|)
   (bind <name> (accept))
   (write (crlf) |What is | <name> |'s address?|)
   (bind <address> (accept))
   (write (crlf) |What is | <name> |'s annual income?|)
   (bind <income> (accept))
   (write (crlf) |How long at current job?|)
   (bind <currentjob> (accept))
   (write (crlf) |How much stock does | <name> | have?|)
   (bind <stock> (accept))
   (write (crlf) |How much savings does | <name> | have?|)
   (bind <savings> (accept))
   (write (crlf) |What is the current credit card balance?|)
   (bind <creditcards> (accept))
   (bind <oti> (compute <income> // 3))
   (bind <osi> (compute <income> // 6))
   (make applicant ^name <name> ^address <address> ^income <income>
         ^currentjob <currentjob> ^stocks <stock> ^savings <savings>
         ^credit <creditcards> ^one-third-income <oti>
         ^one-sixth-income <osi>))
```

After this rule fires, the working memory should contain two working memory elements, one for the phase and one for the applicant. We now need to collect some information about the property that is being purchased. We want this rule to fire only in the application phase, so we will want the pattern `(phase ^name application)` on the left-hand side. We will also want to have a pattern for the applicant, to make sure that this rule fires only after `get-applicant-info` fires. Finally, we will put a negated `property` pattern, to make sure that this rule fires only when a `property` working memory element has not yet been made. In the simplest version of this program, it may not be necessary to have this third pattern, but it is better style.

```
; if we are in the application phase, and there is an applicant but
; no property yet, get the details on the property

(p get-property-info
   (phase ^name application)
   (applicant)
  -(property)
-->
   (write (crlf) |What is the price of the property?|)
   (bind <purchase-price> (accept))
   (write (crlf) |What is the age of the property?|)
   (bind <age> (accept))
   (write (crlf) |What region of the country is the property in?|)
   (bind <region> (accept))
   (write (crlf) |Does the property have septic or sewer?|)
   (bind <waste> (accept))
   (write (crlf) |What is the downpayment?|)
   (bind <dp> (accept))
   (bind <fivep>      (compute <purchase-price> *  .05))
   (bind <tenp>       (compute <purchase-price> *  .10))
   (bind <twentyp>    (compute <purchase-price> *  .20))
   (make property ^price <purchase-price> ^age <age> ^region <region>
         ^waste <waste> ^appraised-value 0 ^money-down <dp>
         ^five-percent <fivep> ^ten-percent <tenp> ^twenty-percent <twentyp>))
```

After these two rules fire, we have collected information about the applicant and the property. We would like the phase to change to `collection`, and if we include the rule `change-phase-to-collection` which was shown above, that will be accomplished.

We ask Maureen what happens during the information collection phase:

> There are obviously two things that we need to collect more information about: the property and the applicants. Let's start with the property. We need to find the average selling price for a home of similar size and age in that region. If we see that this home is significantly more expensive than average for that area, or if the house is selling for more than $153,000, we ask one of our appraisers to go out and see it. If the house is in New England or the Midwest, we ask for a termite inspection, and if it is in the Southeast, we ask for a flood inspection. If the house has its own septic system, we ask for an inspection on that, too.

As a side note, one of the awkward things about OPS5 is the lack of a disjunction (an OR statement) among patterns on the left-hand side of a rule. There is an implicit

AND among patterns, such that *all* left-hand-side patterns must be matched against working memory before the rule enters the conflict set. This lack of disjunction means that we must write three rules instead of one. The problem is not one of efficiency, but that it forces the programmer to say something in an awkward way. There are other rule-based languages (some of which are variations of OPS5) that solve this problem and others, but often at the cost of more complicated syntax, slower performance, or higher purchase cost. Considering OPS5's strengths, it is a small complaint. OPS5 does allow disjunction *within* a pattern, such as in this LHS pattern that matches an applicant named Bob or Bill or Jack or Dave:

```
(applicant ^name <<bob bill jack dave>>)
```

We first write the rules that will order appraisal.

```
(p appraise-when-property-over-limit
    (phase ^name collection)
   {(property ^price > 153000 ^appraised-value 0) <prop>}
-->
    (write (crlf) |Please order an appraisal of the property|)
    (write (crlf) |What is the appraised value?|)
    (bind <appvalue>    (accept))
    (bind <eighty>      (compute <appvalue> *  .80))
    (bind <ninety-five> (compute <appvalue> *  .95))
    (bind <one-twenty>  (compute <appvalue> * 1.20))
    (modify <prop> ^appraised-value <appvalue> ^eighty <eighty>
        ^ninety-five <ninety-five> ^one-twenty <one-twenty>))

(p appraise-when-expensive-for-area
    (phase ^name collection)
    (economy ^region <reg> ^maxprice <ap>)
   {(property ^price > <ap> ^appraised-value 0 ^region <reg>) <prop>}
-->
    (write (crlf) |Please order an appraisal of the property|)
    (write (crlf) |What is the appraised value?|)
    (bind <appvalue> (accept))
    (bind <eighty>      (compute <appvalue> *  .80))
    (bind <ninety-five> (compute <appvalue> *  .95))
    (bind <one-twenty>  (compute <appvalue> * 1.20))
    (modify <prop> ^appraised-value <appvalue> ^eighty <eighty>
        ^ninety-five <ninety-five> ^one-twenty <one-twenty>))

(p order-termite-inspection
   (phase ^name collection)
   (property ^region << midwest newengland >>)
-->
   (write (crlf) |Order a termite inspection|))
```

```
(p order-a-septic-inspection
   (phase ^name collection)
   (property ^waste septic)
-->
   (write (crlf) |Order a septic tank inspection|))
```

We must usually collect more information about the applicant, also. If the amount of stocks owned exceeds 33% of the applicant's salary, or if it exceeds $30,000, we verify this through his stock broker. If he has been at his current job for less than six months, or if he claims income greater than $75,000, we like to verify his salary by seeing a current pay stub or last year's tax return. The same people that downplay their income for the IRS are often inflating it for us! We look at the outstanding balances on the credit cards, also. We do not want to issue the mortgage if the applicant often has credit card balances of more than two months' take-home pay, because people usually put even more things on their credit card in the first three months that they own their new home. So if the current credit card balance is more than a month's pay, we request a payment history from a credit reporting agency.

```
(p verify-if-high-percentage-stocks
    (phase ^name collection)
    (applicant ^one-third-income <oti> ^stocks > <oti>)
-->
    (write (crlf) |Verify stocks with broker|))

(p verify-if-high-stocks
    (phase ^name collection)
    (applicant ^stocks > 30000)
-->
    (write (crlf) |Verify stocks with broker|))

(p new-job
    (phase ^name collection)
    (applicant ^currjob < .5)
-->
    (write (crlf) |Verify employment dates and salary|))

(p high-salary
    (phase ^name collection)
    (applicant ^income > 75000)
-->
    (write (crlf) |Verify salary|))

(p high-credit-cards
    (phase ^name collection)
    (applicant ^credit > <osi> ^one-sixth-income <osi>)
-->
    (write (crlf) |Check credit card payment history|))
```

> You probably see by now why applying for a mortgage takes many weeks. If all the pertinent information were laid out in front of an experienced loan officer, the decision would take about ten minutes. But the real trick is to know what the pertinent information is. It would be a waste of time and money to verify every fact on every application, and to ask for all possible appraisals and inspections of the property. Some of the information has no bearing on the decision in certain cases. Remember, the overall philosophy is that the bank must make a profit by being paid back on these loans. If a loan is not paid back, then we would like to be able to foreclose on the property and get our money back. If the downpayment plus the amount the property is sold for in an auction exceeds the loan amount plus our costs, we have made a profit anyway. An aggressive bank will look for a fairly priced piece of property, or an applicant capable of paying back the loan. In some sense, they do not care which way they make their profit. A more conservative bank will look for both, because an economic downturn could wipe out property values and the applicant's ability to pay back simultaneously. Our bank is on the conservative side.

We next want to move to the categorization phase, which we accomplish like the other phase transitions:

```
(p change-phase-to-categorization
  (phase ^name collection)
-->
  (write (crlf) |Moving to categorization phase| (crlf))
  (modify 1 ^name categorization))
```

Remember that Maureen said the bank categorizes three things: the quality of the downpayment, the quality of the property, and the quality of the applicant's ability to pay. Let's ask her about this process:

> Everything in categorization is relative. A particular house for $100,000 might be a great deal in Boston, but a bad investment in Pittsburgh. Someone earning $50,000 per year could easily handle $1000 per month payments, but could have a tough time with $2500 per month. A 10% downpayment is fine if the house is in an area with rapidly appreciating values, but 30% is not enough if prices are plummeting.
>
> What we want to do in categorization is look at the three most important things (downpayment, property, and income) relative to each other. Some banks use a numeric scheme to label things, while we use a fuzzier system of poor, fair, good, or excellent. At a bank I previously worked at, we had a numeric system that gave a false sense of accuracy in these judgments. It was foolish to say that a person with a 79.15 score was riskier than one with an 80.76 score, because the formulas used to compute the scores were just approximations of the truth anyway. This does not mean that mortgage analysis is just an art, either. There are formulas that are good predictors of how much someone can afford to pay each month. But these formulas must be used as rough guidelines, not absolute indicators. From the articles you've sent me about expert systems, it seems that this is why this is a good application of expert systems.
>
> I'm digressing a bit. Where was I? Oh yes, categorizing. Categorizing the quality of the downpayment is perhaps the simplest of the three. If the downpayment is between 0 and 5% of the appraised value, we call it poor. If it is between 5 and 10%, and the

purchase price is less than $200,000, we call it fair; more than $200,000 makes it poor. If it is between 10 and 20%, we call it good when prices are steady or rising, and fair when prices are falling. A downpayment greater than 20% is excellent when prices are at least steady, and good otherwise.

```
(p less-than-five
   (phase ^name categorization)
   (property ^price <p> ^downpayment < <fp> ^five-percent <fp>)
  {(loan) <loan>}
-->
   (modify <loan> ^downpayment poor))


(p between-five-and-ten-cheap-property
   (phase ^name categorization)
   (property ^price < 200000 ^downpayment {> <fp> < <tp>} ^five-percent <fp>
                             ^ten-percent <tp>)
  {(loan) <loan>}
-->
   (modify <loan> ^downpayment fair))


(p between-five-and-ten-expensive-property
   (phase ^name categorization)
   (property ^price >= 200000 ^downpayment {> <fp> < <tp>} ^five-percent <fp>
                              ^ten-percent <tp>)
  {(loan ^downpayment nil) <loan>}
-->
   (modify <loan> ^downpayment poor))


(p between-ten-and-twenty-good-economy
   (phase ^name categorization)
   (property ^price < 200000 ^money-down {> <tp> < <twp>} ^ten-percent <tp>
                             ^twenty-percent <twp> ^region <r>)
   (economy ^prices << steady rising >> ^region <r>)
  {(loan ^downpayment nil) <loan>}
-->
   (modify <loan> ^downpayment good))


(p between-ten-and-twenty-bad-economy
   (phase ^name categorization)
   (property ^price < 200000 ^money-down {> <tp> < <twp>} ^ten-percent <tp>
                             ^twenty-percent <twp> ^region <r>)
   (economy ^prices falling ^region <r>)
  {(loan ^downpayment nil) <loan>}
-->
   (modify <loan> ^downpayment fair))
```

```
(p over-twenty-good-economy
   (phase ^name categorization)
   (property ^money-down > <twp> ^twenty-percent <twp> ^region <r>)
   (economy ^prices << steady rising >> ^region <r>)
  {(loan ^downpayment nil) <loan>}
-->
   (modify <loan> ^downpayment excellent))

(p over-twenty-bad-economy
   (phase ^name categorization)
   (property ^money-down > <twp> ^twenty-percent <twp> ^region <r>)
   (economy ^prices falling ^region <r>)
  {(loan ^downpayment nil) <loan>}
-->
   (modify <loan> ^downpayment good))
```

We have written rules to categorize downpayments, and now we would like to categorize the property. We ask Maureen to tell us about property:

> Categorizing property is a bit trickier. If the purchase price is less than 80% of appraised value, we call it excellent. But appraisals are a snapshot of prices now, so in a rising market, we call a price up to 95% of appraised value excellent. In a falling market, 80% would just be considered good. If the purchase price is greater than 120% of appraised value in a steady market, we call it poor, unless prices are rising, in which case it is fair. In a falling market, the loan would be out of the question when the purchase price exceeds the appraised value.

```
(p less-than-eighty-percent
    (phase ^name categorization)
   {(property ^price < <eightyp> ^eighty <eightyp> ^home-value nil
        ^appraised-value > 0) <p>}
-->
    (modify <p> ^home-value excellent))

(p less-than-ninety-five-percent
    (phase ^name categorization)
   {(property ^price < <nfp> ^ninety-five <nfp> ^home-value nil
        ^appraised-value > 0 ^region <r>) <p>}
    (economy ^prices rising ^region <r>)
-->
    (modify <p> ^home-value excellent))

(p greater-than-120-rising
    (phase ^name categorization)
   {(property ^price < <otp> ^one-twenty <otp> ^home-value nil
        ^appraised-value > 0 ^region <r>) <p>}
    (economy ^prices rising ^region <r>)
```

```
-->
    (modify <p> ^home-value fair))

(p greater-than-120-steady
    (phase ^name categorization)
   {(property ^price < <otp> ^one-twenty <otp> ^home-value nil
        ^appraised-value > 0 ^region <r>) <p>}
    (economy ^prices steady ^region <r>)
-->
    (modify <p> ^home-value poor))

(p greater-than-100-falling
    (phase ^name categorization)
   {(property ^price < <app> appraised-value > 0 ^home-value nil
        ^region <r>) <p>}
    (economy ^prices falling ^region <r>)
-->
    (modify <p> ^home-value poor))
```

The next phase of the decision process is the most important in some ways, but it is also the easiest. At this point, you have collected and verified all the information that is needed, and you must just look at it and decide what to do. As we mentioned before, a rating of *poor* in any of the categories would automatically rule out the loan at a conservative bank. If any area is *excellent* and there are no *poor*s, then the loan can be accepted. In other cases, we will look for at least two ratings of *good*.

First, let's write a rule that will change the phase for us:

```
(p change-phase-to-evaluate
  (phase ^name categorization)
-->
  (write (crlf) |Changing to evaluation phase| (crlf))
  (modify 1 ^name evaluation))
```

Next, let's write rules to reject a loan when any category is *poor*:

```
(p poor-downpayment
  (phase ^name evaluation)
 {(loan ^status undecided ^downpayment poor) <loan>}
-->
  (modify <loan> ^status rejected)
  (write (crlf) |Rejected because of poor downpayment| (crlf)))

(p poor-property
  (phase ^name evaluation)
  (property ^home-value poor)
 {(loan ^status undecided) <loan>}
-->
  (modify <loan> ^status rejected)
  (write (crlf) |Rejected because of poor home value| (crlf)))
```

```
(p poor-payment-ability
  (phase ^name evaluation)
  (applicant ^payment-ability poor)
 {(loan ^status undecided) <loan>}
-->
  (modify <loan> ^status rejected)
  (write (crlf) |Rejected because of poor payment ability| (crlf)))
```

Let's add three more rules that look for values of `excellent` in any of the three categories:

```
(p excellent-downpayment
  (phase ^name evaluation)
 {(loan ^downpayment excellent ^status undecided) <loan>}
-->
  (modify <loan> ^status accepted)
  (write (crlf) |Accepted because of excellent downpayment| (crlf)))

(p excellent-property
  (phase ^name evaluation)
  (property ^home-value excellent)
 {(loan ^status undecided) <loan>}
-->
  (modify <loan> ^status accepted)
  (write (crlf) |Accepted because of excellent home value| (crlf)))

(p excellent-payment-ability
  (phase ^name evaluation)
  (applicant ^payment-ability excellent)
 {(loan ^status undecided) <loan>}
-->
  (modify <loan> ^status accepted)
  (write (crlf) |Accepted because of excellent payment ability| (crlf)))
```

If there are no `poors` or `excellents`, then we will want at least two `good` ratings:

```
(p good-downpayment-and-property
  (phase ^name evaluation)
  (property ^home-value good)
 {(loan ^downpayment good ^status undecided) <loan>}
-->
  (modify <loan> ^status accepted)
  (write (crlf) |Accepted because of good downpayment and property| (crlf)))

(p good-property-and-payment-ability
  (phase ^name evaluation)
```

```
  (property ^home-value good)
  (applicant ^payment-ability good)
 {(loan ^status undecided) <loan>}
-->
  (modify <loan> ^status accepted)
  (write (crlf) |Accepted because of good property and payment ability|
         (crlf)))

(p good-payment-ability-and-downpayment
  (phase ^name evaluation)
  (applicant ^payment-ability good)
 {(loan ^downpayment good ^status undecided) <loan>}
-->
  (modify <loan> ^status accepted)
  (write (crlf) |Accepted: good payment ability and downpayment| (crlf)))
```

When a bank writes a loan, there are certain precautions that may be taken to prevent loss in case of catastrophe. Let's ask Maureen about that. She says:

> There are basically two things that need to be protected against: harm to the property and harm to the person paying us back. While we of course care about the welfare of our customers, from a business standpoint we are strictly interested in not losing money on any mortgage. In order to do that, we have to insure against certain dangers. If the house is more than 10 years old, and the loan amount exceeds $80,000, we'd like title insurance on the house to guard against claims later on. If there is only a fair or good downpayment, we'd like the borrower to carry enough life insurance to pay back at least 50% of the borrowed amount. For the structure itself, we'd always like adequate coverage against flooding and fire, which means enough to rebuild the house from scratch. This coverage, by the way, is often much less than the purchase price, because the land itself wouldn't be lost in a fire.

First we'll need to change the phase to security. We do this as we did all the other phase changes:

```
(p change-phase-to-security
   (phase ^name evaluation)
-->
   (modify 1 ^name security)
   (write (crlf) |Changing phase to security| (crlf)))
```

Now we add the rules that secure the loan:

```
(p adequate-life-insurance
  (phase ^name security)
  (loan ^status accepted)
  (property ^downpayment  <<fair good>> ^price <p>)
-->
  (bind <ins> (compute <p> / 2))
  (write (crlf) |Borrower must carry $| <ins> | in life insurance| (crlf))))
```

```
(p adequate-house-insurance
  (phase ^name security)
  (loan ^status accepted)
  (property ^appraised-value <value>)
-->
  (write (crlf) |Borrower must carry $| <value>
               | in home insurance| (crlf))))

(p adequate-title-insurance
  (phase ^name security)
  (loan ^status accepted)
  (property ^age >= 10 ^price {<p> >= 80000})
-->
  (write |Borrower must have title insurance with coverage of $| <p> (crlf)))
```

Finally, we need a final rule that fires when no others can:

```
(p final-rule
  {(phase ^name security) <ph>}
-->
   (write (crlf) |We're done with the application process| (crlf))
   (modify <ph> ^name done))
```

Let's run the program for a simple case, and see how it works. Note that the watch facility is turned on when we begin OPS5, so the rule names and the matching working memory time tags will be printed in capital letters as each rule fires.

```
% ops5
> (load "/condor/c0/jcm/chap5/code.ops")
> (make start 1)
> (run)

1. INITIALIZE-THINGS 1
2. GET-APPLICANT-INFO 4

What is the applicant's name? John

What is  JOHN 's address? Chicago

What is  JOHN 's annual income? 75000

How long at current job? 3.5

How much stock does  JOHN  have? 12000

How much savings does  JOHN  have? 65000

What is the current credit card balance? 2300
```

```
3. GET-PROPERTY-INFO 4 9

What is the price of the property? 245000

What is the age of the property? 23

What region of the country is the property in? midwest

Does the property have septic or sewer? sewer

What is the downpayment? 76000

4. CHANGE-PHASE 4

Moving to collection phase

5. APPRAISE-WHEN-EXPENSIVE-FOR-AREA 12 6 10

Please order an appraisal of the property
What is the appraised value? 220000

6. ORDER-TERMITE-INSPECTION 12 14

Order a termite inspection

7. CHANGE-PHASE-TO-CATEGORIZATION 12

Moving to categorization phase

8. OVER-TWENTY-GOOD-ECONOMY 16 14 6 3
9. GREATER-THAN-120-RISING 16 14 6
10. CHANGE-PHASE-TO-EVALUATE 16

Changing to evaluation phase

11. EXCELLENT-DOWNPAYMENT 22 18

Accepted because of excellent downpayment

12. CHANGE-PHASE-TO-SECURITY 22

Changing phase to security

13. ADEQUATE-TITLE-INSURANCE 26 24 20

Borrower must have title insurance with coverage of $ 245000
```

```
14. ADEQUATE-HOUSE-INSURANCE 26 24 20

Borrower must carry $ 220000  in home insurance

15. FINAL-RULE 26

We're done with the application process

end -- no production true
 41 productions (231 // 457 nodes)
 15 firings (28 rhs actions)
  7 mean working memory size (8 maximum)
  2 mean conflict set size (4 maximum)
 19 mean token memory size (25 maximum)
NIL
> (quit)
```

5.4 SUMMARY

In this chapter, we described a relatively complex set of guidelines that determine mortgage qualification. We showed how the constraints of the problem can be mapped into OPS5 working memory element declarations and rules.

We showed techniques for grouping rules, which makes the program easier to debug and comprehend. We discussed features that could be added to the basic system, showing OPS5's flexibility.

5.5 PROBLEMS

1. Add rules that make sure the user types reasonable values. For instance, if the user types in a credit card balance that is greater than the annual salary, you should verify both figures. Another check would be to make sure that no numbers are negative. Also, if the downpayment were much larger than the sum of the savings and stock, you could ask the user to verify the downpayment.
2. Check to see if the current set of rules covers all possible cases of property price, region, and downpayment. If not, extend the rule set with rules that fill in the gap.
3. The current rule set prompts for information about credit card debt, but does not make use of that information in its decision. Decide what you would do with credit card debt if you worked for the bank, and write a rule to reflect this policy.
4. Some rules have `(loan ^downpayment nil)` as a left hand side pattern. Change one of them to `(loan)` and see what happens when the rule fires. Explain why.
5. Two rules, `poor-payment-ability` and `excellent-payment-ability`, make use of the attribute `payment-ability` in working memory elements of type `applicant`, however no rules in this set put values into that attribute. Using

the information from the bank officer in the text (or your own judgment), decide what factors contribute to an applicant's payment ability, and add several rules to reflect that policy.

6

THE RETE ALGORITHM

6.1 OPS5 INTERNALS

One of the most interesting features of OPS5 is the representation it uses internally for the rules and working memory. The scheme it uses is very efficient in use of memory and processing, and makes it possible to use OPS5 on relatively large problems. It is not essential to know how the internals work in order to use OPS5, just as one does not need to know much about engines in order to drive a car. You may safely ignore this chapter if you have no interest, but if you are the kind of person who is curious, you will be rewarded with understanding an elegant algorithm.

The internal data structure used to represent both rules and working memory in OPS5 is called the *Rete* (pronounced "ree-tee") net. The word *rete* means net, web, or neural network, so the phrase *Rete net* is actually a bit redundant, but commonly used.

The Rete net was created by Charles Forgy as part of his Ph.D. work at Carnegie-Mellon University. In his thesis, he describes a predecessor to OPS5, called OPS2. The syntax of OPS2 differs a bit from OPS5, but the languages are fairly similar. Previous production system interpreters had been built, and Forgy observed that there were two aspects of their execution that could be exploited to build a faster interpreter. The first property is *temporal redundancy*, which means that working memory changes relatively slowly over time. Forgy observed that working memory might typically contain scores of working memory elements, yet only a few would be added or removed with each rule firing. Likewise, the set of rules that are able to fire (called the conflict set) might also change slowly over time in a typical rule set. Thus, it might prove easier to compute the *difference* between the previous conflict set and the current one, rather than computing the current conflict set from scratch. The second property that can be exploited is *structural similarity*. What this means is that in most sets of rules, there are some common patterns on left-hand sides. For example, a rule might be a subset of another rule, or two rules might differ just by one condition element. In these cases, matching each rule individually against working memory would be clearly inefficient, because certain parts of the matching process would be shared by more than one rule.

A common programming technique in Artificial Intelligence is the discrimination net. There is nothing very mysterious about a discrimination net. Suppose we wanted to come up with a list of questions to discriminate between brands of cars. We could ask whether the car is made in the United States. We might ask the number of cylinders the car has. We might ask whether the car costs more than 20,000 dollars. The discrimination net's performance would clearly depend on the group of cars we were trying to choose from. If the group contained no more than one car for each distinct set of answers, we could discriminate each of the cars by just using these questions. If more than one car shared a distinct set of answers, we would have to augment the discrimination network by asking more questions.

In its simplest form, a discrimination net is a tree. Each node of the tree has a test which can be applied to a concept. The next branch traversed depends upon the results of the test. In this simple case, the tree has no "memory," and each test begins from scratch. OPS5 builds a discrimination net when a set of rules is read in. This discrimination net tells the interpreter which rules are eligible to fire. The OPS5 discrimination net has nodes with "memory;" that is, nodes can store results of previous tests in order to speed up the discrimination.

6.2 HOW THE NETWORK IS BUILT

A Rete net is an extended form of discrimination net. While a discrimination net has a question or test at each junction, a Rete net actually has a very small program to be run, possibly including some data. A new Rete net is built each time a set of rules is read in. In fact, the left-hand sides of the rule are essentially compiled into a Rete net.

Since some rules often share patterns with other rules, the Rete net will grow more slowly than it would if each rule were completely independent. The structure of the Rete net does not change after the last rule is read in (unless the `build` command is used), but the values at the nodes in the net may change when additions to or deletions from working memory are made. For simplicity, think of `make` as an addition to working memory, `remove` as a deletion from working memory, and `modify` as a deletion followed by an addition. The running of an OPS5 program, then, is the process of operating on this Rete net.

There are many types of nodes in the Rete net. We will first discuss some of the types, and then show an example of how they might be used.

- **&BUS**. There is only one node of this type in a Rete net. It is always the top node. When this node is processed, it initializes some variables.

- **&AND**. This node type has a left and a right input, each with a memory. When a token comes in either node, and it is the first to arrive, it is stored in the memory. When the second token comes in, the two are compared according to a series of tests, and if the tests are satisfied, a token leaves the node.
- **&TWO**. This node type has one input, and sends the input to two outputs, essentially performing a fork.
- **&NOT**. Allows tokens to pass if none of the elements in its memory cause any of the tests to fire.
- **&P**. This node type is always a leaf in the Rete net. It contains the name of a production or productions. When a token comes into this node type, the productions are added to or taken out of the conflict set.
- **&ANY**. Compares the token type with a list of constants. If any match, then the token is passed on.
- **TEQA**. Takes an index and a constant atom, and compares a piece of the token with it, passing on the token if they are equal. Similarly, there are nodes called **TLTN**, **TEQN**, **TNEN**, and so on; these test for less than, equal to, and not equal to for numeric constants.

Let's see how a Rete net might be built. We will use the following rules:

```
(literalize car brand model doors color)
(literalize driver name age skill)

(p disqualify-underage-drivers
   (driver ^name <n> ^age < 16)
-->
   (write (crlf) <n> | is too young to drive!| (crlf))
   (remove 1)
)

(p old-guys-drive-sports-cars
   (car ^brand {<<jaguar ferrari porsche>> <brand>} ^model <model>)
   (driver ^name <n> ^age > 50)
-->
   (write (crlf) <n> | can drive the | <brand> | | <model> (crlf))
)

(p almost-anyone-can-drive-a-bug
   (car ^brand vw ^model bug ^color <c>)
   (driver ^name <n> ^age > 16)
-->
   (write (crlf) <n> | can drive a bug| (crlf))
)
```

The `literalize` sets up a canonical order for each type of working memory element. This ordering maps each field of the working memory element to a number, which speeds up the matching later. Therefore, if the canonical order is (car brand model doors color), a (make car ^model pinto ^color red) is transformed to add car nil pinto nil red. Since the number of doors is always in the fourth position, the tests can quickly compare the fourth element to a constant. This is a case of trading off storage space for faster execution.

After the first rule is read in, the Rete net looks like Example 6.1. The &BUS node is the top node, and there is a TEQA test to see if the working memory element is of type driver. Next, the value of field 2 (the driver's name) is stored in variable *c1*. The value of location 3 (the driver's age) is tested to see if it is less than 16. At the leaf, there is a &P node which adds or the rule disqualify-underage-drivers to the conflict set.

Example 6.1. Rete net after first rule

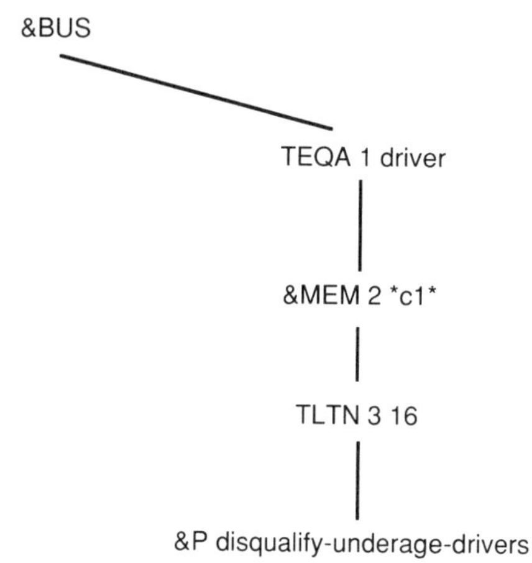

After reading in the second rule, there is a test to see if the working memory element is of type car. The second field is tested to see if it is equal to jaguar, ferrari, or porsche, and the value is stored in *c2*. A test on the driver's age is added to see if it is over 50, and the results of the two branches are joined with an &AND node.

Example 6.2. Rete net after second rule

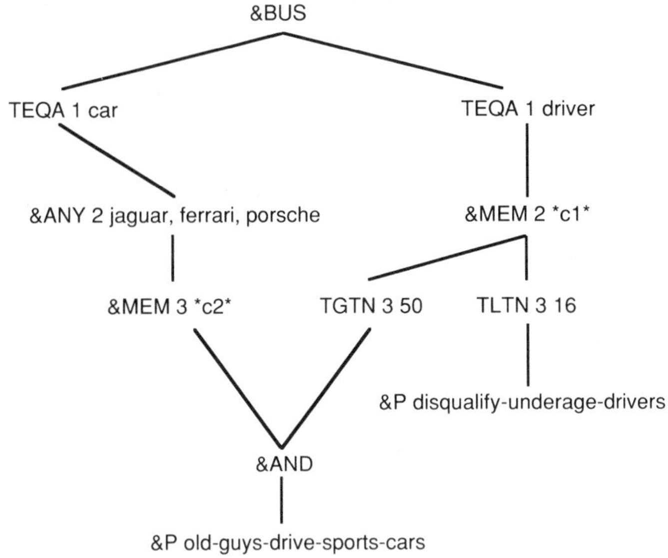

The third rule adds similar features to the Rete net, with the final network shown below.

Example 6.3. Rete net after third rule

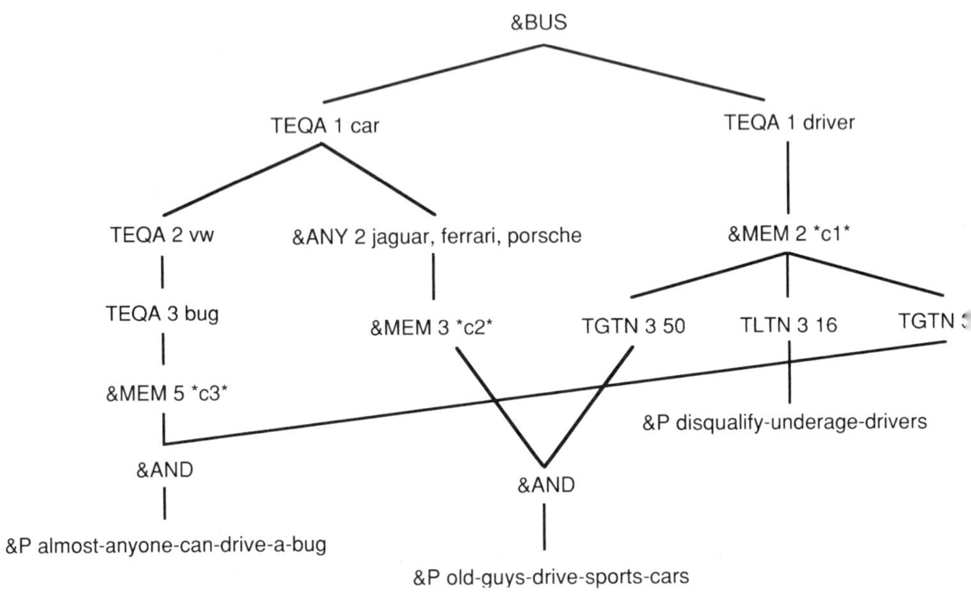

Even in this small set of rules with a small set of working memory element types, there is some sharing of tests in the network. For large rule sets, this overlap is even more beneficial. In general, the Rete net grows quite slowly as more rules are added to it, because there is often so much structural similarity between rules.

6.3 PASSING TOKENS

Suppose we now add some working memory elements to the system. We create some cars and drivers:

```
(make driver ^name sean ^age 11 ^skill good)
(make driver ^name eileen ^age 29)
(make driver ^name stan ^age 55)
(make car ^brand vw ^model bug ^doors 2 ^color white)
(make car ^brand jaguar ^model xjs ^color black)
```

The following diagrams show what happens as the five `make`s are performed. First, an underage driver is made, which enables a rule to fire.

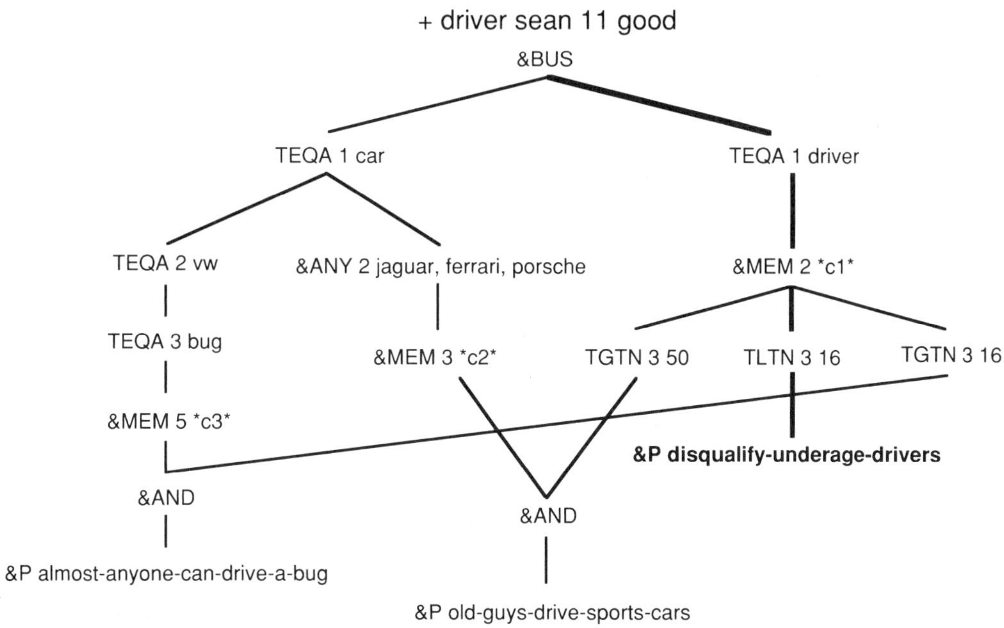

When the right-hand side of the enabled rule is eventually executed, it will pass the token `remove driver sean 11 good` down the top of the network, and the rule will become disabled again.

Next, a legal driver is created. Tokens are propagated all the way to the leftmost `&AND` node, but since no car is yet available, no rules are enabled.

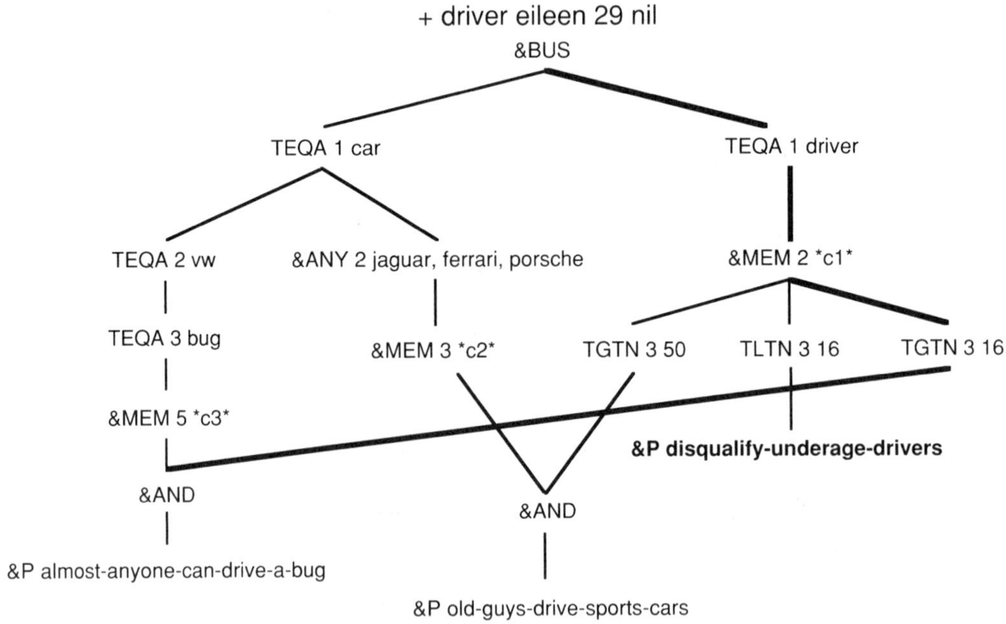

Now, an older driver is created. This time, tokens are propagated down several paths, because the driver is both over 55 and over 16. Still, no further rules are enabled, since there are still no cars available.

We make our first car a two-door white VW bug.

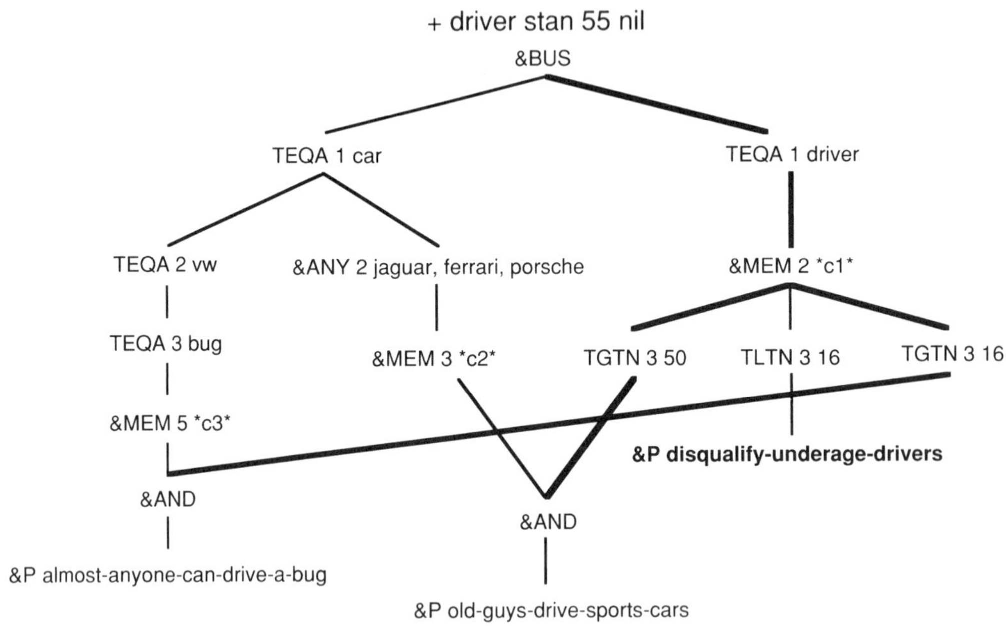

Now there are three sets of rules and data in the conflict set. Sean is enabling the disqualify rule, and Stan and Eileen both enable the bug rule with the same VW bug.

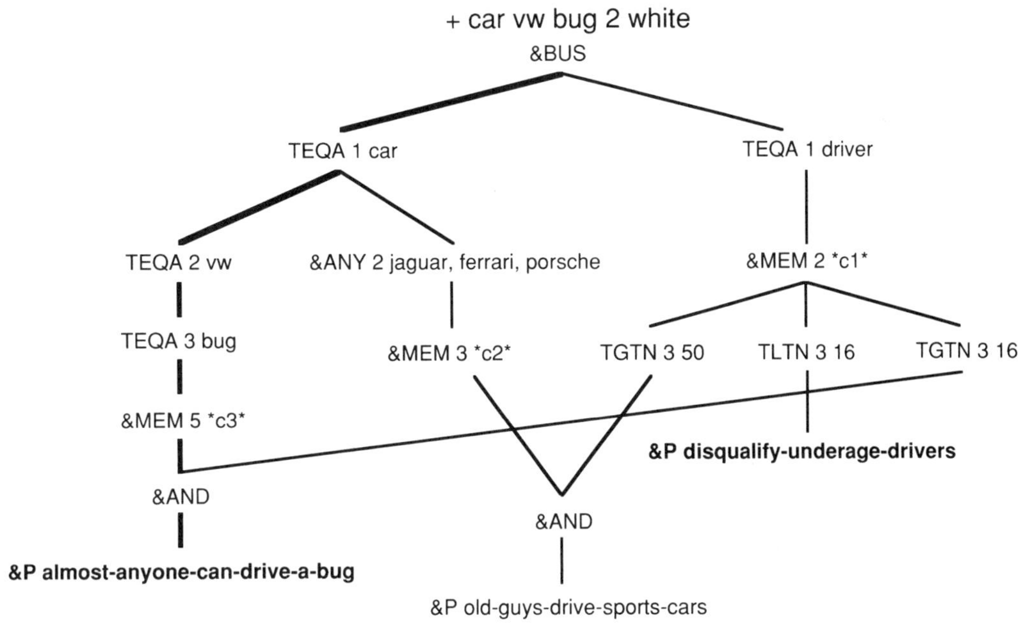

Finally, we create a Jaguar.

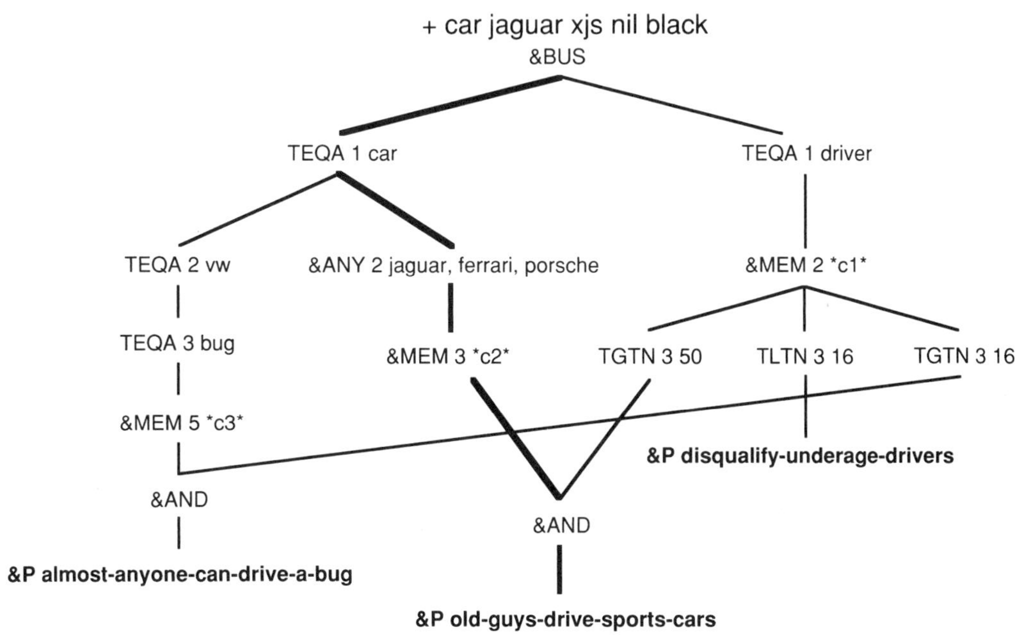

There are now four instantiations in the conflict set: one of `disqualify-under-age-drivers`, matching Sean, one of `old-guys-drive-sports-cars`, matching Stan and the Jaguar, and two of `almost-anyone-can-drive-a-bug`, matching on the VW bug, once with Stan, and once with Eileen.

6.4 SUMMARY

A Rete net is a machine that accepts as input changes in working memory, and produces as output the changes in the conflict set. With the possible exception of the `build` command, the network is built at the the beginning of a session, and its structure stays static for the duration of a session. Tokens are passed down from the &BUS node through the various tests until a &P node is reached. At this point, a production is added to or taken out of the conflict set.

The primary consideration in OPS5 programming is getting a program that works; however, efficiency issues can be important. As in other programming languages, a slight change in algorithm or code might result in a huge change in performance because of the way the language is compiled or interpreted.

If one knows how a Rete net works, one can make some predictions about the performance of certain rule sets. As might be expected, a shallow Rete net will be faster to traverse than a deep one. A rule set where there are many patterns on the left-hand side will result in a broader, shallower tree, and therefore one that is faster to traverse. Without knowing about the Rete net, one might guess that adding rules to a rule set would always make pattern matching slower. If one considers how the Rete net works, one can see that adding rules with different types of working memory elements can actually speed up the matching process, because certain tests will fail at a high level in the tree.

The Rete net has been used in other rule-based interpreters, such as ART, OPS83, and YAPS. Universities have looked at implementations of Rete that take advantage of certain types of hardware, such as parallel processors. There are improvements of the Rete algorithm, such as the TREAT algorithm by Daniel Miranker at Columbia University. The main point is that production systems would be useless for all but toy problems if the Rete algorithm had not been invented. Brute force pattern matching of rules against working memory would be out of the question in any real system. By understanding the Rete algorithm, you will not only understand OPS5 better, but you may also be lucky enough to discover applications of Rete nets to other problems in Artificial Intelligence.

7

ADVANCED TOPICS

7.1 DYNAMIC RULE BUILDING

In all computer programming, situations can arise that call for changes in program design. We are all aware of the problems that occur during debugging when a piece of software may be modified extensively so that it performs properly. Then there is the maintenance phase when the software is patched or enhanced so that it will continue to be useful. The structure of OPS5 allows the designer to build one form of self-maintenance: dynamic rule building. When used correctly, dynamic rule building can save time because the program does not have to stop while being reprogrammed. On the other hand, though, dynamic rule building poses the problem of testing the new rules. We advise that simplicity is the best policy and that new rules added to a working program should maintain a structure consistent with the rules already in the program.

The example of dynamic rule building that we will demonstrate relates to the loan qualifying program from previous chapters. Assume that a new category has been added to the program: different loan types. Also, assume that each applicant will be evaluated for each category. Example 7.1 shows how a rule might be written to perform this evaluation.

Example 7.1. Fixed-rate rule

```
(p fixed_rate
  {<app> (applicant ^name <nam> ^requested <amount> )}
  {<mort> (mortgage_type ^name fixed_rate ^rate <rt> ^mlen <len>)}
```

```
-->
  (make mort_types ^name fixed_rate ^appl <nam>
        ^month_rate (compute ((<amount> * <rt>) + <amount> ) // <len> ))))
```

A simple formula is used to determine the monthly payments that the applicant would have to pay given the amount of the loan, the interest rate, and the length of the loan. A class of "mortgage types" is then filled with this information along with the applicant's name. Let us assume that when the program was written there were only fixed-rate mortgages, but that the programmer or banking expert knew that different types of mortgages were going to be available in the future. One solution to this problem would be to schedule a programmer to be available so that when any new mortgage appears, the programmer can adjust the program. Another solution is to design into the program the ability for the program to build new rules as new mortgage types appear. Example 7.2 is a short OPS5 program that will build a new rule for a new mortgage rate.

Example 7.2. Example of rule building

```
; RULE BUILDING PROGRAM FOR OPS5

; Program to show how to build a new rule dynamically.
(literalize mortgage_type name rate mlen )
(literalize applicant name requested )
(literalize mort_types name appl month_rate)

; Rule that builds new rules for new mortgage types
(p new_mortgage_type_new_rule
   (start)
-->
   (write (crlf)|Enter new mortgage type... |)
   (bind <nmt> (accept))
   (write (crlf)| Enter interest rate ... |)
   (bind <irate> (accept))
   (write (crlf)|  Enter minimum length ...|)
   (bind <ml> (accept))
   (make mortgage_type ^name <nmt> ^rate <irate> ^mlen <ml> )
 (build \ \ <nmt> {<app> (applicant ^name <nam> ^requested <amount>)}
   {<mort>(mortgage_type ^name \ \ <nmt>
              ^rate <rt>
              ^mlen <len>)}
 -->
   (make mort_types ^name \ \ <nmt>
              ^appl <nam>
 ^month_rate (compute ((<amount> * <rt>)
              + <amount> )
              // <len>))))

; Rule to load WM
(p load_wm
```

```
    (mortgage_type)
-->
    (make applicant ^name john-smith ^requested 50000)
    (make applicant ^name tom-tucker ^requested 7500))
```

The program will query the user for three things: the name of the new mortgage type (which will also become the name of the rule), the interest rate of the new mortgage type, and the length of the mortgage. Notice that the rule in Example 7.1 has been included within the rule `new_mortgage_type_new_rule` and it is prefaced by the `build` command instead of `p`. The `build` command tells OPS5 to dynamically build the rule with the name and code that follow. The `build` command requires the new rule name as the first argument. For example, if the `build` command was written as `(build test ...)`, a rule named `test` would be created when the `build` was executed. Note that the argument is taken literally and is not evaluated. However, in line 1 of Example 7.2 the `build` command uses a variable that represents the name of a new mortgage type as typed by a user. The difference between what `build` takes as literal and as evaluated, e.g., a variable, is defined by the symbol \\ . Notice that in the example, lines 2 and 6 also use the \\ symbol to denote evaluation of the argument. This ensures that the newly input name, rate, and length will be fixed to the new rule being created. Example 7.3 shows the runtime output of the program. Note that the rule `adjustable_rate` does not exist until after the rule `new_mortgage_type_new_rule` is fired. After the rule is fired, then the `build` command is invoked as an action command and the rule is built.

Example 7.3. Adjustable-rate rule is built

```
; Part 1 - Shown with (watch 3)
Dribble file build.drb opened
: (load|buildex.ops|)
**
: (watch 3)
: (make start)

=>CS: 0. new_mortgage_type_new_rule  1
: (pm adjustable_rate)
'adjustable_rate' is not a production

: (run)
1. new_mortgage_type_new_rule  1

Enter new mortgage type... adjustable_rate

   Enter interest rate ... .17
   Enter minimum length ... 48

=>WM: 2:   (mortgage_type ^name adjustable_rate ^rate 0.17 ^mlen 48)
=>CS: 1. load_wm  2
```

```
2. load_wm  2
=>WM: 3:   (applicant ^name john-smith ^requested 50000)
=>CS: 2. adjustable_rate  3 2
=>WM: 4:   (applicant ^name tom-tucker ^requested 7500)
=>CS: 2. adjustable_rate  4 2
3. adjustable_rate  4 2
=>WM: 5:   (mort_types ^name adjustable_rate ^appl tom-tucker
            ^month_rate 182.8125)
4. adjustable_rate  3 2
=>WM: 6:   (mort_types ^name adjustable_rate ^appl john-smith
            ^month_rate 1218.75)
No production true
: (wm)

6:   (mort_types ^name adjustable_rate ^appl john-smith
      ^month_rate 1218.75)
5:   (mort_types ^name adjustable_rate ^appl tom-tucker
      ^month_rate 182.8125)
4:   (applicant ^name tom-tucker ^requested 7500)
3:   (applicant ^name john-smith ^requested 50000)
2:   (mortgage_type ^name adjustable_rate ^rate 0.17 ^mlen 48)
1:   (start)
: (pm adjustable_rate)
(p adjustable_rate
{<app> (applicant ^name <nam> ^requested <amount> )}
{<mort> (mortgage_type ^name adjustable_rate ^rate <rt> ^mlen <len> )}
-->
(make mort_types ^name  adjustable_rate ^appl <nam>
^month_rate (compute ((<amount> * <rt> )+ <amount>) //<len>)))

: (dribble-end)

; Part II-  Shown with no watch
Dribble file build.drb opened

: (load|buildex.ops|)
    **
: (make start)
: (pm adjustable_rate)
'adjustable_rate' is not a production
: (run)

Enter new mortgage type... adjustable_rate

    Enter interest rate ... .17

    Enter minimum length ...48
```

```
No production true
: (wm)
6:   (mort_types ^name adjustable_rate ^appl john-smith
      ^month_rate 1218.75)
5:   (mort_types ^name adjustable_rate ^appl tom-tucker
      ^month_rate 182.8125)
4:   (applicant ^name tom-tucker ^requested 7500)
3:   (applicant ^name john-smith ^requested 50000)
2:   (mortgage_type ^name adjustable_rate ^rate 0.17 ^mlen 48)
1:   (start)
: (pm adjustable_rate)
(p adjustable_rate
{<app> (applicant ^name <nam>
                  ^requested <amount> )}
{<mort> (mortgage_type ^name  adjustable_rate
                       ^rate <rt> ^mlen <len> )}
-->
(make mort_types ^name  adjustable_rate ^appl <nam>
      ^month_rate (compute ((<amount> * <rt>) + <amount>) // <len>)))

: (dribble-end)
```

Building rules dynamically is a complicated task and a few warnings should be presented here:

1. A newly built rule cannot access any data in WM that was present before the rule was built. This means that the rules that must be built dynamically should be built earlier in the program than any data that they need. Alternatively, all the data can be stored in a file before the rules are built and then working memory can be refilled with the data after the rules are created.
2. There is no easy way of ascertaining if a newly built rule is working properly after it has been built dynamically. You can run test cases prior to the use of the program, but when the actual program is running, you have to make sure that error checking is done for erroneous input that would crash the program.
3. The instances for using the `build` option in OPS5 have to be identified and well thought out. The previous case was obviously contrived to demonstrate the `build` operation and may not be the best way to perform the new mortgage-type checking. One must weigh the increased complexity and program correctness in relation to the gains that the `build` option will give an OPS5 program.

The OPS5 `build` command gives a great deal of power to the expert system environment, but it also creates problems that are hard to deal with when working in such a complex area. The basic approach that we recommend is to keep it simple. Dynamic rule building has an overhead cost that more times than not will outweigh the benefits.

7.2 SIMULATING CERTAINTY FACTORS

When people make complex decisions, they are not always completely sure of their conclusions. When an expert system offers advice or makes a decision, it is sometimes desirable to have a quantifier associated with the end result. This quantifier is often called a *certainty factor* (CF) and a certainty factor indicates how certain the program is that an answer is true. Obviously, the meaning of *true* is related directly to the process that determines the certainty factors. An example of a CF determination is demonstrated in the automobile diagnosis program in Chapter 8. Certainty factors are usually given a range where the lowest number of the range corresponds to "certain that a conclusion is not true," while the highest number of the range corresponds to "certain that a conclusion is true." In the automobile diagnosis program, the range of the CFs is between -1 and +1, with a 0 meaning that true or false certainty cannot be determined from the present set of facts. Example 7.4 shows the relationships among the rules, facts, and CFs of the program.

Example 7.4. Relationships of certainty factors in the rule

```
(a)  This are how the CF factors are related in the
     Automobile Diagnosis Program:

       (1) gas smell- strong=.7  normal=.0  none=-.2
       (2) lights-  dim=.3  normal=.1
       (3) fuel filter-  clogged=.8  not-clogged=.0
       (4) battery cables-  loose=.5  corroded=.7  normal=.0
       (5) starter-  no-crank=.5  slow-crank=.5  normal=.2  grind=.6
       (6) temperature-  >40=.0  40>t>30=.1  30>t>10=.2  10>t>0=.3
       (7) gas gauge-  empty=.8  not-empty=.1
```

Example 7.5. Certainty factors for the auto diagnosis program

```
Rule1:  Car flooded (gas smell CF minus fuel filter CF minus gas gauge CF)

Rule2:  Empty gas tank (gas gauge CF minus gas smell CF minus fuel filter CF)

Rule3:  Starter malfunctioning (starter CF plus temperature CF)

Rule4:  Fuel filter clogged (fuel filter CF minus gas smell CF minus gas
gauge CF)

Rule5:  Battery cables in disrepair (battery cables CF plus lights CF minus
starter CF minus temperature CF)

Rule6:  Battery is dead (starter CF plus lights CF plus temperature CF minus
cables CF)
```

```
Rule7: Starter malfunctioning (starter CF plus lights CF minus fuel filter
CF minus gas gauge CF)

Rule8: Choke is stuck (starter CF plus temperature CF minus gas smell CF
minus gas gauge CF minus fuel filter CF)
```

`Rule1` starts with the CF for `gas smell` as the main certainty determiner. Then the condition of the fuel filter is subtracted from this because if the filter is clogged, then the engine cannot be flooded. The condition of the gas gauge is also subtracted because if there is no gas in the gas tank, then the engine cannot be flooded. For example:

GAS SMELL CF	FUEL FILTER CF	GAS GAUGE CF	RULE 1 CF
.7	0	.1	+.6
.7	.8	.1	-.2
.7	.8	.8	-.9
.7	0	.8	-.1

Note that the only positive certainty that the engine is flooded is when there is a strong smell of gas and the fuel filter is not clogged and there is gas in the tank. A certainty factor of .1 for the gas gauge reading takes into account that the gauge might be wrong; therefore, `Rule1` will be fairly certain (+.6) that the engine is flooded but not absolutely certain (+1). Example 7.6 is a transcript of the runtime output of the automobile diagnosis program and shows some of the different conclusions and certainties that can be obtained from the program.

Example 7.6. A consultation session

```
(dribble-start exauto.drb)
: (load|exauto.ops|)
****#****#****#****#****#****#***
: (watch 0)

: (make start)

: (run)

 *********************************************
 AUTO CONSULTATION PROGRAM VERSION TWO

This program will analyze your car problems by asking questions about
the functioning of specific areas of your automobile. Please type in
one of the words that follows the three dots in each question. Any
other input will produce erroneous results.

question 1: Gasoline odor is ...none normal strong ?  strong
question 2: Headlights are ...dim normal ?  dim
question 3: Fuel filter is ...clogged not-clogged ?  clogged
```

```
question 4: Battery cables are ...loose corroded normal ?  loose
question 5: Starter cranking is ...no-crank slow-crank normal grind ?
            grind
question 6: Outdoor temperature is ?  32
question 7: Gas gauge reading is ... empty not-empty ?  not-empty

CONCLUSIONS:

***** CF  0.7 *****
Diagnosis is that the starter is malfunctioning.
Treatment is replace starter.

***** CF  0 *****
Diagnosis is that the fuel filter clogged.
Treatment is to replace fuel filter.

***** CF  0.1 *****
Diagnosis is that the battery cables are in disrepair.
Treatment is to clean and tighten battery cables.

***** CF  -0.2 *****
Diagnosis is that car is flooded.
Treatment is to wait ten minutes then try starting
or depress accelerator to the floor while starting.

**** RUN PROGRAM AGAIN ...Y or N ?  y

AUTO CONSULTATION PROGRAM VERSION TWO

This program will analyze your car problems by asking questions about
the functioning of specific areas of your automobile. Please type in
one of the words that follows the three dots in each question. Any
other input will produce erroneous results.

question 1: Gasoline odor is ...none normal strong ?  normal
question 2: Headlights are ...dim normal ?  normal
question 3: Fuel filter is ...clogged not-clogged ?  not-clogged
question 4: Battery cables are ...loose corroded normal ?  normal
question 5: Starter cranking is ...no-crank slow-crank normal grind ?
            normal
question 6: Outdoor temperature is ?  0
question 7: Gas gauge reading is ... empty not-empty ?  empty

CONCLUSIONS:

***** CF  8.299999 *****
Diagnosis is that the starter is malfunctioning.
Treatment is replace starter.
```

```
***** CF  0.8 *****
Diagnosis is that there is no fuel in gas tank.
Treatment is to put gas in tank.

***** CF  0.7 *****
Diagnosis is that the starter is malfunctioning.
Treatment is replace starter.

***** CF  0 *****
Diagnosis is that the fuel filter clogged.
Treatment is to replace fuel filter.

***** CF  0.1 *****
Diagnosis is that the battery cables are in disrepair.
Treatment is to clean and tighten battery cables.

***** CF  -0.2 *****
Diagnosis is that car is flooded.

Treatment is to wait ten minutes then try starting or depress accelerator
to the floor while starting.

**** RUN PROGRAM AGAIN ...Y or N ?  y
```

Example 7.7. Another session

```
AUTO CONSULTATION PROGRAM VERSION TWO

This program will analyze your car problems by asking questions about
the functioning of specific areas of your automobile. Please type in
one of the words that follows the three dots in each question. Any
other input will produce erroneous results.

question 1: Gasoline odor is ...none normal strong ?  none
question 2: Headlights are ...dim normal ?  dim
question 3: Fuel filter is ...clogged not-clogged ?  clogged
question 4: Battery cables are ...loose corroded normal ?  normal
question 5: Starter cranking is ...no-crank slow-crank normal grind ?
            no-crank
question 6: Outdoor temperature is ?  20
question 7: Gas gauge reading is ... empty not-empty ?  not-empty

CONCLUSIONS:

***** CF  -8.3 *****
Diagnosis is that the fuel filter clogged.
Treatment is to replace fuel filter.
```

```
***** CF  8.299999 *****
Diagnosis is that the starter is malfunctioning.
Treatment is replace starter.


***** CF  0.8 *****
Diagnosis is that there is no fuel in gas tank.
Treatment is to put gas in tank.


***** CF  0.7 *****
Diagnosis is that the starter is malfunctioning.
Treatment is replace starter.


***** CF  0 *****
Diagnosis is that the fuel filter clogged.
Treatment is to replace fuel filter.


***** CF  0.1 *****
Diagnosis is that the battery cables are in disrepair.
Treatment is to clean and tighten battery cables.


***** CF  -0.2 *****
Diagnosis is that car is flooded.
Treatment is to wait ten minutes then try starting or depress accelerator
to the floor while starting.

**** RUN PROGRAM AGAIN ...Y or N ?  n


No production true
: (dribble-end)
```

The determination of certainty in an expert system is a complicated process. The method above works if the number of rules are limited and the conclusions of the system can be projected. But as an expert system becomes more complicated and more rules are added, then the maintenance of certainty factors can be problematic and add expensive overhead. Many systems (such as OPS83) have built-in facilities for using certainty factors and the reader should study them if certainty factors are important to an application. *Mycin* and *Prospector* are two expert systems that have used certainty factors successfully. The limitation of these two systems is that they used specific models and based their CF determinations on these models and on the user's opinion of certainty. The problem with certainty evaluations is that they are usually statistically based and rely greatly on precious action and reaction. An expert system designed to handle new situations may not have such a database of facts or the expert around to guide it. Therefore, much work is still being done in the field of certainty factors and there has yet to be a standard approach.

7.3 INTERFACING WITH OTHER LANGUAGES

OPS5 was designed to perform rule-based operations such as matching, inference chaining, and rule firing. It is not a convenient language to use for other operations associated with computers (i.e., files, I/O, complex math, complex data structures). It would be ideal if the OPS5 language allowed the programmer to perform all the basic computer operations in another language and then call the OPS5 environment only when it is needed. The next generation of OPS (see Chapter 9) takes a step in that direction but OPS5 is limited to external system calls. The language that will be used in this section to demonstrate the external access is Common LISP. This is the language that the public domain OPS5 is written in. If your particular OPS5 uses another language, we suggest that you read this section and then consult your user's manual for further information on interfacing with external routines. Example 7.8 shows the names and descriptions of specific functions used by OPS5 when accessing external routines. These functions will be explained as they are used in the following examples of external routines. Example 7.9 is a program that uses LISP to perform arithmetic. The program is the LQ example with the first rule modified so that the values for `halfincome-plus-savings` and `debt-plus-halfdebt` are returned by a LISP macro.

Example 7.8. Functions used to interface with LISP

NAME	ARGUMENT	DESCRIPTION
$value	single argument	Changes a LISP value to OPS5, used to return a result value.
$varbind	single argument	Changes an OPS5 value to LISP, used to select a value from an OPS5 argument(s).
$parameter	single argument	Changes an OPS5 value to LISP, uses an integer argument as pointer to element(value) in result buffer.
$parametercount	none	Returns length of the result buffer.
$reset	none	Initializes the result buffer and resets pointer to initial value.
$assert	none	Loads the values of the result buffer into WM.
$tab	single argument	Positions the argument at the next position in the result buffer.
$litbind	single argument	Returns pointer to attribute (argument).

Example 7.9. Lisp macro calls

```
; program name: LQL1.ops        date:7/1/88
;
; Test program to demonstrate a LISP macro calls from a the public domain
; OPS5 program.

; define LISP macros as external to the OPS5 program
; the LISP macros have been placed last in the source code
;
(external incsav)
(external debthalf)

(literalize applicant   name
                        ss-num
                        income
                        savings
                        debt
                        halfincome-plus-savings
                        debt-plus-halfdebt)

(make start)

(p instantiate-WM

   {<st>(start)}
    -->
        (remove 1)

        (make applicant ^name           John-Smith
                        ^ss-num         04742997
                        ^income         60000
                        ^savings        50000
                        ^debt           15000
        ^halfincome-plus-savings (incsav 60000 50000)
        ^debt-plus-halfdebt  (debthalf 15000)

        (make applicant ^name           Tom-Tucker
                        ^ss-num         nil
                        ^income         40000
                        ^savings        25000
                        ^debt           100000
                        ^halfincome-plus-savings  (incsav 40000 25000)
                        ^debt-plus-halfdebt  (debthalf 100000) ))

;----------------------------------------------------------------
;LISP macros
;
```

```
1: (defmacro incsav (&body args)
2:      ($value (+ (/ ($varbind (car args)) 2)
3:      ($varbind (cadr args)))))
;
4: (defmacro debthalf (&body arg)
5:      ($value (+ (/ ($varbind (car arg)) 2)
6:      ($varbind (car arg)))))
```

The way that OPS5 accesses the external macros is by simply using their names and arguments as the value assigned to an attribute. The arguments that are passed are the income, savings, and debt. Note that the very first lines of code in the program declare that the two LISP macros used are "external." This must be done for any routine that is external to the OPS5 environment and that is going to be used by OPS5. The math performed by the LISP macros `incsav` and `debthalf` is the same math performed by the OPS5 `compute` action. This section is only intended to guide the reader through the intricasies of passing/returning data using external LISP routines. It is up to the reader to learn about the power of LISP and create the design specific routines that will enhance their OPS5 programs. Example 7.9 uses LISP macros that return a single value. When the macro is called, all the arguments are passed by OPS5 as a string and that is why in lines 1 and 4 the LISP command `&body` is used to assign the argument string to the variables `args` and `arg`. The LISP macros need special commands to access the OPS5 values. In lines 2, 3, 5, and 6 the command `$varbind` is used to get the OPS5 data. Note that the argument associated with the `$varbind` is a command that isolates a value in a list. For example, in line 2,

```
($value (+ (/ ($varbind (car args)) 2)
```

The first operation that occurs is the `(car args)` function which returns the value of the first element in the list `args`. This value is bound to the LISP environment by `$varbind` and the LISP math is performed. Remember that the argument list that was passed when the `incsav` macro was first called looked like this:

```
(60000  50000)
```

The list above represents the income and savings of the applicant John Smith. The macro `incsav` will divide the income by two and add the result to the savings. This is what we want for the value of `halfincome-plus-savings`. The final value is then stored in an OPS5 "result" buffer by `$value` and the result buffer is returned as the value of the attribute `halfincome-plus-savings`. Macros work well when a single resulting value is all that is required. But for file manipulation and input and output operations, a LISP function is needed.

Example 7.10 represents an OPS5 program that will call a LISP function. The purpose of this program is to demonstrate how a LISP function can receive a list of OPS5 data and how a LISP program can load WM with values.

Example 7.10. Lisp function calls

```
; program name: LQL2.ops      date:7/1/88
;
; Test program to demonstrate a LISP function calls
; from a the public domain OPS5 program.
;
;---------------------------------------------------
; define LISP functions as external to the OPS5 program
; the LISP functions have been placed last in the source code

(external lfunction)

;---------------------------------------------------------

(literalize initial data )
(literalize applicant  name
                       income
                       savings
                       debt
                       halfincome-plus-savings
                       debt-plus-halfdebt)

(vector-attribute data)

;--------------------------------------------------------------

(p instantiate-WM

   {<st> (start)}
   -->
         (remove 1)
         (make initial  ^data   John-Smith 60000 50000 15000)
         (make initial  ^data   Tom-Tucker 40000 25000 100000))

(p LISP-makes
   {(initial) <int>}
   -->
    (call lfunction (substr <int> 1 inf) )

;---------------------------------------------------------------
;LISP function calls
;
  (defun lfunction ()
   (do ( (cdex 1 (+ 1 cdex))
1:       (wmlist () (cons ($parameter cdex) wmlist)) )
2:     ( (equal cdex (+ 1 (parametercount)))
3:       ($reset )
```

```
4:        ($value 'applicant)
5:        ($tab   'name)
6:        ($value (cadr (reverse wmlist)))
7:        ($tab   'income)
8:        ($value (caddr (reverse wmlist)))
9:        ($tab   'savings)
10:       ($value (cadddr (reverse wmlist)))
11:       ($tab   'debt)
12:       ($value (car (cddddr (reverse wmlist))))
13:       ($tab   'halfincome-plus-savings)
14:       ($value (incsav (caddr (reverse wmlist)))
15:                       (cadddr (reverse wmlist))) )
16:       ($tab   'debt-plus-halfdebt)
17:       ($value (debthalf  (car (cddddr (reverse wmlist)))
18:       ($assert))
          )
        )
      )

   (defun incsav (in sa)
     (+ (/ in 2) sa) )

   (defun debthalf (db)
     (+ (/ db 2) db) )

  (make start)
```

Note that the external function also has to be declared as external at the top of the OPS5 program. The way to access an external LISP function is simple by calling it. This is demonstrated in the rule **LISP-makes** as shown below:

```
(call lfunction (substr <int> 1 inf))
```

The function name is `lfunction` and the argument passed is a list that represents the vector attribute `data` of the element class `initial`. This was done so to demonstrate how a list can be passed to a function. Note that the function is defined without arguments. This is because OPS5 uses a special buffer (referred to as the result buffer) and accessed by the command `$parameter` within the function. The purpose of the LISP function `lfunction` is to demonstrate two aspects of the result buffer operation: first, how an OPS5 program can send a list to a LISP function and second, how an external function can load values into WM. This function is contrived to demonstrate the above concepts and should only be used as an example of this. It should not be viewed as efficient interaction between OPS5 and LISP! It would be more appropriate for the function to input values from a terminal or a file and allow the full computing power of LISP to perform error checking on the data. Line 1 in the function is set up to use the initialization section of the LISP `do` function to load all the values that are being passed from OPS5 into the list `wmlist`. The way that OPS5 and LISP communicate is through a result buffer. This is a bidirectional buffer and since it will be used to pass values to WM, the values that are being received must be saved (otherwise, they will be lost when the buffer is used again). The term `cdex` is the count variable used in the loop and the function (`$parameter cdex`) gives the value at that location in the result buffer. Therefore, this function loops through the whole list that was passed by the rule `LISP-makes` and stores each element in a LISP list called `wmlist`. Line 2 tells the loop when to stop by checking to see if the count variable `cdex` is equal to the length of the result buffer (this length is given by the `$parametercount` function). Note that the loop is set up to increment one more time past the length of the buffer. This is to make sure that the last element is stored on the `wmlist` before the loop ends. Now all the data is stored in the list `wmlist` and the `result` function can be used again to communicate between the OPS5 and LISP without losing any data. Line 3 is the `$reset` command, which initializes the OPS5 result buffer. It sets the buffer pointer to the first location in the buffer. Line 4 loads a literal name into the result buffer (this will be the class name `applicant`). Line 5 moves (tabs) the result buffer pointer to the next location in the buffer and loads the attribute `name` into the buffer. Line 6 loads the value of the first element of the list `wmlist` into the result buffer. This is done by using

```
($value (cadr (reverse wmlist)))
```

The `wmlist` contains the following values the first time it is called by `LISP-makes`:

```
(100000 25000 40000 tom-tucker initial)
```

Notice that it is in reverse order (that is the way it was unloaded from the result buffer). Line 6 reverses the list, gets the value `tom-tucker` from the list, and stores the value on the result buffer (`$value` does the actual loading). The same procedure is used in lines 7 through 12. Lines 14, 15, and 17 use LISP functions to perform math. This was done to demonstrate that nested functions could be used in an external LISP call. Line 18 is needed to pass the result buffer to WM. Note that the result buffer will retain the data until it is reset; then the data will be lost. The `$assert` command can be used multiple times along with the others in Example 7.8. Example 7.11 shows the input and output as the program in Example 7.10 is executed.

Example 7.11. Running the program

```
>(load "lql2.ops")
**
>(wm)
1:(start)
>(watch 2)
2
>(run)
1: instantiate-wm 1
<=wm: 1: (start)
```

```
=>wm: 3: (initial ^data  john-smith    60000  50000  15000)
=>wm: 4: (initial ^data  tom-tucker    40000  25000  100000)
2: LISP-makes 4
=>wm: 5: (applicant ^name tom-tucker ^income 40000
  ^savings 25000 ^debt 100000 ^halfincome-plus-savings 45000
  ^debt-plus-halfdebt 150000)
3: LISP-makes 3
=>wm: 6: (applicant ^name john-smith ^income 60000
  ^savings 50000 ^debt 15000 ^halfincome-plus-savings 80000
  ^debt-plus-halfdebt 22500)
end -- no production true
>(wm)
3: (initial ^data  john-smith    60000  50000  15000)
4: (initial ^data  tom-tucker    40000  25000  100000)
5: (applicant ^name tom-tucker ^income 40000  ^savings 25000
   ^debt 100000 ^halfincome-plus-savings 45000
   ^debt-plus-halfdebt 150000)
6: (applicant ^name john-smith ^income 60000 ^savings 50000
   ^debt 15000 ^halfincome-plus-savings 80000
   ^debt-plus-halfdebt 22500)
>
```

A skilled programmer can use LISP to handle all major computing operations while using OPS5 strictly for inferencing and rule-based operations. This is recommended only for someone who is familiar with both LISP and OPS5.

7.4 INTERFACING WITH C

Interfacing with C is similar to LISP is many ways. In fact the Sienna version of OPS5 even uses the same commands with the first character changed from a $ to a _ (see Example 7.12).

Example 7.12. Calls used to interface to C

NAME	ARGUMENT	DESCRIPTION
_value	single argument	Changes a LISP value to OPS5, used to return a result value.
_varbind	single argument	Changes an OPS5 value to LISP, used to select a value from an OPS5 argument(s).
_parameter	single argument	Changes an OPS5 value to LISP, uses an integer argument as pointer to element(value) in result buffer.
_parametercount	none	Returns length of the result buffer.

_reset	none	Initializes the result buffer and resets pointer to initial value.
_assert	none	Loads the values of the result buffer into WM.
_tab	single argument	Positions the argument at the next position in the result buffer.
_litbind	single argument	Returns pointer to attribute (argument).
_cvaf	single argument	Convert atom (argument) to float.
_cvan	single argument	Convert atom (argument) to long integer.
_cvas	single argument	Convert symbolic atom (argument) to string.
_cvfa	single argument	Convert float(argument) to argument.
_cvna	single argument	Convert long integer (argument) to atom.
_cvsa	string argument	Convert string (argument) to atom.
_eql	double argument	Test 2 atoms for equality.
_ifile	single argument	Returns an input file pointer.
_ofile	single argument	Returns an output file pointer.
_intern	string argument	Make a string (argument) into a symbol.

Notice that there are some new commands included in this list. They pertain to conversions and file I/O. The Sienna OPS5 C interface passes all OPS5 arguments as atoms and that is why the conversion commands are needed. The examples presented in Example 7.13 and Example 7.14 demonstrate basic interaction between OPS5 and C. It is beyond the scope of this book to show more complex operations. The reader can investigate the Sienna documentation for further information on C external calls. The Sienna student version of OPS5 does not allow the user to develop external C programs. The examples that are included here have been compiled and linked using the "full strength" Sienna OPS5. The purpose of these examples is to demonstrate the capability of OPS5 to use the external C environment. If you need a working C interface, then you should get in touch with Sienna about their industrial OPS5. The program in Example 7.13(a) is an OPS5 program that is similar to the LISP program (from the previous section) that uses macro calls to pass and receive data.

Example 7.13. Calling a C function from OPS5

```
(a) OPS5 program that calls a C external function,  passes
    it values and receives a single value back.

; program name: LQC1.ops     date:9/12/88

; Test program to demonstrate C function calls

; Define C functions as external to the OPS5 program.
; The C functions have been placed in the opsiml.c file.

(external INCSAV)
(external DEBTHALF)

(literalize applicant   name
                        ss-num
                        income
                        savings
                        debt
                        halfincome-plus-savings
                        debt-plus-halfdebt)

(literalize loan-action          dissapprov
                                 approv)

(p instantiate-WM

   {<st>(start)}
   -->
        (remove 1)

        (make applicant ^name            John-Smith
                        ^ss-num          04742997
                        ^income          60000
                        ^savings         50000
                        ^debt            15000
                        ^halfincome-plus-savings (INCSAV 60000 50000)
                        ^debt-plus-halfdebt  (DEBTHALF 15000)

        (make applicant ^name            Tom-Tucker
                        ^ss-num          nil
                        ^income          40000
                        ^savings         25000
                        ^debt            100000
                        ^halfincome-plus-savings  (INCSAV 40000 25000)
                        ^debt-plus-halfdebt  (DEBTHALF 100000)))

 (make start)
 ;
```

```
; PROGRAM END
```

(b) C program to receive values from an OPS5 call and
will return a single value.

```
/*   Program to Test C Interface to OPS5

     Program File Name: opsim1.c
     Coder: P. Sherman           Date: 9/12/88

The functions in this program will be called by the OPS5 program
LQC1.OPS . Two arguments will be sent to u_incsav and they are: income
& savings.  One argument will be sent to u_debthalf and it is: debt.
The functions will return one argument each.

These are external files needed by the C program.

*/

#include "stdio.h"
#include "ops5.h"         /* needed by ops5 */

extern void incsav();
extern void debthalf();

OPS_EXTERNF ops_externals[] =
        {{"INCRSAV",incsav},
         {"DEBTHALF",debthalf},
        };

/*
 incsav: figures out pay back base by dividing income in half and
         adding savings to it
*/

void incsav (inc,sav)
         OPS_ATOM inc,sav;
   {long int i = _cvan (inc);
    long int s = _cvan (sav);
        i = (i / 2) + s;
    _value(_cvna(i)); }

/*
 debthalf: figures out max debt allowed by dividing debt in half and
           adding debt to it
*/
```

```
void debthalf (debt)
 OPS_ATOM debt;
   {long int d = _cvan (debt);
        d = (d / 2) + d;
    _value(_cvna(d)); }

/*
END OF PROGRAM
*/
```

Example 7.13(b) is the code for the C external routines. Example 7.14(a) is an OPS5 program that sends a string to an external C program. Example 7.14(b) is the code for the C program that will receive a string and then perform a `make` to WM. This does the same action as the second LISP program in the previous section.

Example 7.14. Sending a string to C

```
(a) OPS5 program that will send a string to a C program.

; test opsbook program
;
; program name: LQC2.ops        date:9/12/88
;
; Test program to demonstrate a C function call
; that will perform an evaluation and then access WM
;
;---------------------------------------------------
; define C function as external to the OPS5 program
; the C function have been placed in the file opsim2.c

(external CFUNCTION)

;---------------------------------------------------------

(literalize initial data )
(literalize applicant name
                      income
                      savings
                      debt
                      halfincome-plus-savings
                      debt-plus-halfdebt)

(vector-attribute data)

;------------------------------------------------------------

 (p instantiate-WM
    {<st>(start)}
```

```
   -->
    (remove 1)
    (make initial   ^data   John-Smith 60000 50000 15000)

    (make initial   ^data   Tom-Tucker 40000 25000 100000))

 (p C-makes
   {(initial) <app>}
   -->
    (call CFUNCTION (substr <app> data inf)))

  (watch 3)
  (make start)

; PROGRAM END
```

(b) C program that will receive a string from OPS5 and
will perform a "make" to WM.

```
/*   Program to Test C Interface to OPS5

     Program File Name: opsim2.c
     Coder: P. Sherman     Date: 9/12/88

     The functions in this program will be called by the OPS5 program
     LQC2.OPS . An array will be passed to the C function which will
     initial data, perform the "incsav" and "debthalf" evaluations via a C
     call, and the store the data in WM.

    These are external files needed by the C program
*/

#include "stdio.h"
#include "ops5.h" /* needed by ops5*/

extern void cfunction();

OPS_EXTERNF ops_externals[] =
{{"CFUNCTION",cfunction},
 { NULL, NULL }
};

/* C function that will input an array from the OPS5 program
   and store it individual variables "parm" 1 to 4.Then it will
   store this information in WM as the applicant class. Note that
   it will evaluate "incsav" & "debthalf" before they are stored
   in WM.
*/
```

```
void cfunction ()
{
OPS_ATOM incsav2(), debthalf2();
OPS_ATOM parm1, parm2, parm3, parm4;

parm1 = _parameter(1);
parm2 = _parameter(2);
parm3 = _parameter(3);
parm4 = _parameter(4);

_reset();
_value(_cvsa("APPLICANT"));
_tab(_cvsa("NAME"));
_value(parm1);
_tab(_cvsa("INCOME"));
_value(parm2);
_tab(_cvsa("SAVINGS"));
_value(parm3);
_tab(_cvsa("DEBT"));
_value(parm4);
_tab(_cvsa("HALFINCOME-PLUS-SAVINGS"));
_value(incsav2(parm2,parm3));
_value (debthalf2(parm4));
_tab(_cvsa("DEBT-PLUS-HALFDEBT"));
_value(debthalf2(parm4));
_assert();
 return;
 }

/*
   incsav: figures out payback base by dividing income in half and add
   savings to it
*/

   OPS_ATOM incsav2 (inc,sav)
   OPS_ATOM inc,sav;
  {
    long int i = _cvan(inc);
    long int s = _cvan(sav);

    i = (i / 2) + s;
    return(_cvna(i));
  }

  /*
      debthalf: figures out max debt allowed
        by dividing debt in half and add debt to it
```

```
    */

    OPS_ATOM  debthalf2(debt)
    OPS_ATOM debt;
    {
      long int d = _cvan(debt);

      d = (d / 2) + d;
      return(_cvna(d));
    }

  /*
    END OF PROGRAM
  */
```

It must be pointed out again that a good grasp of both OPS5 and C are mandatory before trying to write efficient external functions. The above programs introduce the concepts of external function calls but proper, efficient use of external calls comes from experience. The requirements of the initial problem (expertise that you are trying to encapsulate in an expert system) will be the determining factor as to what can be incorporated as an external function. Being able to recognize these determining factors is something that comes with experience. For example, large data bases that need to be accessed and changed around would best be done in a language other than OPS5. The same goes for extensive user interaction where error checking and correction must be performed. Other areas might be extensive sorting, complex math operations, and complex array manipulations.

7.5 SUMMARY

The topics covered in this chapter demonstrate that a rule-based expert system can perform many advanced operations. The most important are the interfacing with other languages because this gives the system a window to other languages that can enhance the operation of the production system. The backward chaining is useful for problems such as diagnosis, but care should be taken in the initial choice of expert system shell. If the problems are all of the backward chaining type, then a language that favors backward chaining (such as Prolog) would be advised. The certainty section, the dynamic rule building section, and the explanation section deal with more complicated, but important, issues. Further reading in expert system design is suggested if these topics interest you.

7.6 PROBLEMS

1. Describe two situations (different from the one already mentioned in the chapter) where dynamic rule building would be appropriate.

2. Write an OPS5 rule to perform dynamic rule building for one of the situations in problem 1.
3. Describe other ways of keeping track of the certainty of a conclusion. Show how each new approach could be coded in OPS5 rules. What is the overhead for each approach, and how accurate do you think it will be? Justify your answers.
4. Write an OPS5 program that will use another language (C or LISP) to perform the following:
    - Quicksort on an array of data.
    - Factorial of a number.

8

CASE STUDIES

The following programs demonstrate some of the basic techniques used in rule-based expert systems. The first case study demonstrates an interactive diagnostic program that uses a simple certainty factor strategy to rate solutions. The second case study is a real estate evaluation program that matches listings (represented as data in a file) with the needs of a prospective builder. The third case study demonstrates a synthesis type of program that will input data from a file, manipulate the data, and then output the updated data back out to a file. An explanation of each program is presented along with the source code. These case studies are meant to be used as demonstrations of OPS5 techniques. They may not be the best ways to solve the specific problems, and they may not even be the best way to use OPS5, but the authors feel that demonstration through example is the best way to solidify theoretical concepts.

8.1 AUTOMOBILE STARTING DIAGNOSIS

This case study deals with automobile engine starting problems. The disk that accompanies this book contains the source code for this program in a file called `EXAUTO.OPS`. Note that the first page is comments and description pertaining to the operation of the program. We assume a limited number of engine ailments: engine flooding, no gas, clogged fuel filter, dead battery, broken starter, or stuck choke. There are certain conditions that must be checked that relate to specific problems: smell of gas, illumination of the lights, condition of the fuel filter, condition of the battery cables, noise the starter makes, the outside temperature, and the reading on the gas gauge. The relationships between the ailments and the conditions are represented indirectly in the OPS5 rules.

The certainty factors (CFs) were derived from a basic knowledge that an engine expert had. For example, the certainty that the engine is flooded depends on the strong smell of gas less the condition of the fuel filter (clogged means that no fuel can get to the carburetor and flood the engine) less the reading of the gas gauge (an empty tank also means that no fuel can flood the engine). Therefore, if there was a strong smell of gas (CF = 0.7) and the fuel filter was not clogged (CF = 0.0) and the gas gauge read not empty (CF = 0.1—note that this is not zero because it is possible that the gauge could be broken), then the certainty that the engine were flooded is 0.7 − 0.0 − 0.1 = 0.6 (a very strong indication that the engine should be checked for flooding). The other ailments are handled in much the same way. Example 8.1 represents the output of the program when it is run. The first rule that fires is the `INIT` rule, and it queries the user for the conditions. After the questions are answered, then `SETCF` rules are fired as needed. The decision rules are then fired as needed, displaying the solution or solutions that are determined and presenting a certainty with each solution. The reader should try entering different combinations to see if the CFs are always correct. Note that a class named `route` is used so that only a specific group of rules are eligible to fire at a given time. The last group of rules that will fire are the rules that determine if the program should run again. They will either restart the program after clearing memory, or they will let the program end with no productions true.

The data structures set up for this program are as follows:

1. The record to hold the value of the conditions and the values of the certainty factors.

CLASS	ATTRIBUTES (CONDITIONS)	ATTRIBUTES (CERTAINTY FACTORS)
evidence	gasoline-odor	cf1
	headlights	cf2
	fuel-filter	cf3
	battery-cables	cf4
	starter-cranking	cf5
	outdoor-temperature	cf6
	gas-gauge-reading	cf7

2. The record to hold the value of the answer input from the user as to whether the user wishes to run the program again.

CLASS	ATTRIBUTES
continue	answer

3. The record to hold the value of the route (which group of rules are to fire).

CLASS	ATTRIBUTES
route	next

The rules used in this program are described as follows:

```
1. (p INIT ...)
```

This rule asks the user about seven conditions of the automobile engine. Then the rule loads working memory with the input values and sets the route attribute to `cf`. The `cf` route value enables the certainty factor rules to fire and evaluate the certainty factors.

```
2. (p SETCF10 ...)
```

This rule sets the CF for a strong odor of gas.

```
3. (p SETCF11 ...)
```

This rule sets the CF for a normal odor of gas.

```
4. (p SETCF12 ...)
```

This rule sets the CF for no odor of gas.

```
5. (p SETCF20 ...)
```

This rule sets the CF for dim headlights.

```
6. (p SETCF21 ...)
```

This rule sets the CF for normal headlights.

```
7. (p SETCF30 ...)
```

This rule sets the CF for a clogged fuel filter.

```
8. (p SETCF31 ...)
```

This rule sets the CF for normal fuel filter.

```
9. (p SETCF40 ...)
```

This rule sets the CF for loose battery cables.

```
10. (p SETCF41 ...)
```

This rule sets the CF for corroded battery cables.

```
11. (p SETCF42 ...)
```

This rule sets the CF for normal battery cables.

```
12. (p SETCF50 ...)
```

This rule sets the CF for dead starter.

```
13. (p SETCF51 ...)
```

This rule sets the CF for a slow cranking starter.

```
14. (p SETCF52 ...)
```

This rule sets the CF for a normal starter.

```
15. (p SETCF53 ...)
```

This rule sets the CF for a grinding starter.

```
16. (p SETCF60 ...)
```

This rule sets the CF for an outdoor temperature between 41 and 50 degrees.

```
17. (p SETCF61 ...)
```

This rule sets the CF for an outdoor temperature between 31 and 40 degrees.

```
18. (p SETCF62 ...)
```

This rule sets the CF for an outdoor temperature between 11 and 30 degrees.

```
19. (p SETCF63 ...)
```

This rule sets the CF for an outdoor temperature between 1 and 9 degrees.

```
20. (p SETCF60 ...)
```

This rule sets the CF for an outdoor temperature between 41 and 50 degrees.

```
21. (p SETCF70 ...)
```

This rule sets the CF for an empty gas tank.

```
22. (p SETCF71 ...)
```

This rule sets the CF for a not-empty gas tank.

```
23. (p leave_cf_module ...)
```

This rule is used to change the route variable to `output`. This rule is reached only after all the SETCF rules have fired because the only attribute it has in the LHS is the route class, while the other SETCF rules have an additional attribute to contend with (see Chapter 3).

```
24. (p flooded ...)
```

This rule outputs the diagnosis and certainty for a flooded engine.

```
25. (p out_of_gas ...)
```

This rule outputs the diagnosis and certainty for an empty gas tank.

```
26. (p starter_problems ...)
```

This rule outputs the diagnosis and certainty for an obviously bad starter.

```
27. (p clogged_filter ...)
```

This rule outputs the diagnosis and certainty for a clogged fuel filter.

```
28. (p loose_cables ...)
```

This rule outputs the diagnosis and certainty for battery cables in disrepair.

```
29. (p battery_problems ...)
```

This rule outputs the diagnosis and certainty for a dead battery.

```
30. (p bad_starter ...)
```

This rule outputs the diagnosis and certainty for a not-obviously-bad starter.

```
31. (p choke_stuck ...)
```

This rule outputs the diagnosis and certainty for a stuck choke.

```
32. (p leave_output_module ...)
```

This rule changes the route variable to the `ag` value (short for "again").

```
33. (p AGAINQ ...)
```

This rule will question the user whether they want to run the program again.

```
34. (p AGAINY ...)
```

This rule will clear WM and prepare the system to run again.

Example 8.1. Auto diagnosis program run

```
OPS5 > (make start)
OPS5 > (run)

**********************************************
AUTO CONSULTATION PROGRAM VERSION TWO

This program will analyze your car problems by asking questions about
the functioning of specific areas of your automobile. Please type in
one of the words that follows the three dots in each question. Any
other input will produce erroneous results.

***** QUESTION 1 *****
Gasoline odor is ...none normal strong ?   strong

***** QUESTION 2 *****
Headlights are ...dim normal ?   dim

***** QUESTION 3 *****
Fuel filter is ...clogged not-clogged ?   not-clogged

***** QUESTION 4 *****
Battery cables are ...loose corroded normal ?   loose

***** QUESTION 5 *****
Starter cranking is ...no-crank slow-crank normal grind ?   normal

***** QUESTION 6 *****
Outdoor temperature is ?   45

***** QUESTION 7 *****
Gas gauge reading is ... empty not-empty ?   not-empty


CONCLUSIONS:

***** CF  0.000000e+000 *****

Diagnosis is that the battery is discharged.

Treatment is to charge or replace battery.


***** CF  6.000000e-001 *****
```

```
Diagnosis is that car is flooded.

Treatment is wait ten minutes then try starting
or depress accelerator to the floor while starting.

***** CF  6.000000e-001 *****

Diagnosis is that the battery cables are in disrepair.

Treatment is to clean and tighten battery cables.

---------------------------------------------------------------

**** RUN PROGRAM AGAIN ...Y or N ?   n

end -- no productions true
```

8.2 GROCERY BAGGING (SYNTHESIS) PROGRAM

This case study deals with reading items from a file and grouping them. It is from Patrick Winston's book, *Artificial Intelligence*, and is used with his permission. The items are grocery products and the groupings represent shopping bags. Therefore, the items must be classified according to size, weight, and temperature. Example 8.2 is the input file containing the grocery items. The program will input this file and then it will check to see if there are pairs of specified items: peanut butter and jelly, ice cream and whipped cream. If one half of the pair exists, then the other half is added to the items list. This is done in the rules `STORE-NEW-ITEMS1-PEANUT-BUTTER` and `STORE-NEW-ITEMS2-WHIPPED-CREAM` through all the rules that have the route variable `rvalue` equivalent to `check`. The program continues on, first bagging large items, making special note of bottles and creating new bags when more than six large items are in a bag. Next, the medium-sized items are bagged, with twelve maximum to a bag. Last to be bagged are the small items. They can go into large bags with no bottles up to twelve items, and they can go into medium-sized bags up to eighteen items. The disk accompanying this book contains the source code for this program in the file `EXBAGIT.OPS` and Example 8.3 represents the runtime display for the items in `FILE.T`.

Example 8.2. Grocery bagging data

```
file.t
# of items  index pointers
48             0 0

item name                container       size/wgt     temp  quant flag
peaches......           plastic-bag       medium        no      1    nil
```

```
milk.........        cardbrd-box   medium   no    3   nil
apples.......        plastic-bag   medium   no    1   nil
cookies......        cardbrd-box   medium   no    2   nil
hamburger....        plastic-bag   small    no    2   nil
beer.........        bottle        large    no    2   nil
froz-waffles.        cardbrd-box   small    yes   1   nil
cheese.......        plastic-bag   small    no    3   nil
stop
```

The data structure setup for this program is as follows:

1. The record to hold the values of an individual item. Bag-id, processed, and bagged-q are flags that relate the condition of the item.

```
CLASS          ATTRIBUTES
temp-item       item
container
size
frozen
quantity
bag-id
processed
bagged-q
```

2. The record to hold the flag values of an individual bag as it is being filled.

```
CLASS          ATTRIBUTES
temp-bag        item-num
bag-type
contain
full
iterate
```

3. The record to hold the values of an individual item that will be stored in a bag.

```
CLASS          ATTRIBUTES
store           sitem
scontain
ssize
sfroz
squan
sbag
```

4. The records to hold the flags that tell if the header has been printed out, the bag content has been printed, the present type of bag, what is being processed, and count/status of two loops.

```
CLASS                  ATTRIBUTE(S)
header                  printed

present-bag-type        pbtype

item-or-bag             i-or-b

count                   cnt
loop

loop-val                iterate2
next-rvalue
iarray-val
```

5. The records to represent individual arrays for five bags.

```
CLASS               ATTRIBUTES
bag1-items-array      b1dex
b1count
b1i-array

bag2-items-array      b2dex
b2count
b2i-array

bag3-items-array      b3dex
b3count
b3i-array

bag4-items-array      b4dex
b4count
b4i-array

bag5-items-array      b5dex
b5count
b5i-array
```

6. The records to hold the flags, list of pointers, indexes for the item arrays, and the bag arrays.

```
CLASS                  ATTRIBUTES
item-array              next-avail-slot
iindex
iterindex
item-vector

bag-array               bindex
bcount
```

```
bcurrent
bag-vector

bagged-items-output-array  bio-index
                           bio-array
bagged-rout                brarray
```

7. The records to hold the value of the route (which group of rules are to fire) and the route array.

```
CLASS           ATTRIBUTES
rout-array       rindex
rout-id-vector

rout             rvalue
```

The rules used in this program are described as follows:

```
1.  (p INIT ...)
```

This rule will load WM records with all the initial condition values. It will also change the route variable to `in-file`.

```
2. (p FILL-ITEM-ARRAY-FROM-FILE ...)

   (p FILL-ITEM-VECTOR-FROM-FILE ...)

   (p CLOSE-ITEM-ARRAY-FILE ...)
```

These rules deal with opening the data file `file.t`, reading the index flags from it, loading the class `item-array` with the data from data file `file.t`, closing the file `file.t`, and changing the route variable to `firstprint`. Note how the class count is used to create a repeating loop until the word `stop` is input from the file.

```
3.  (p OUTPUT-START-HEADER1 ...)

    (p OUTPUT-START-HEADER2 ...)

    (p OUTPUT-START-HEADER3 ...)
```

These rules deal with printing out a header to the screen, printing out the contents of the file that was just read, and printing out a header that sets up the screen for the bag array printout and changes the route variable to `startout`. Note that a flag class is used to make sure that this is the first printout.

```
4.  (p OUTPUT-START-ARRAY1 ...)
```

This rule dumps the bag1 contents to the screen to show that the bags are empty. It also changes the route variable to `check`.

```
5. (p CHECK-INITIAL ...)

   (p CHECK-FINISHED-LEAVE ...)

   (p CHECK-TO-ADD-ON-JELLY ...)

   (p CHECK-TO-ADD-ON-WHIPPED-CREAM ...)

   (p CHECK-TO-CONTINUE ...)
```

These rules set up the search parameters that will institute searches for missing items. The searches will continue until all items have been checked, then the route variable will be changed.

```
6.  (p SEARCH-FOR-ITEM-PAIR-0 ...)

    (p SEARCH-FOR-ITEM-PAIR-1 ...)

    (p SEARCH-FOR-ITEM-PAIR-2 ...)
```

These rules actually perform the search for the missing items.

```
7.  (p STORE-NEW-ITEMS1-PEANUT-BUTTER ...)

    (p STORE-NEW-ITEMS2-WHIPPED-CREAM ...)
```

These rules will load the items into WM if they are found to be missing.

```
8. (p FILL-TEMP-ITEMS ...)

   (p FILL-TEMP-BAGS ...)

   (p TEMP-BAG-CATCH-BOTTLE ...)

   (p TEMP-BAG-CATCH-ALL ...)
```

These rules will load the temporary arrays with an item at a time and set the iteration flag when the correct conditions are present in the temp arrays.

```
9.  (p FULL-BAG1 ...)

    (p FULL-BAG2 ...)
```

These rules fire if the specific bags are full. They store the items that are in the full bag and initialize another bag.

```
10. (p BAG1-ITEMS-IN-BAG ...)

    (p BAG2-ITEMS-IN-BAG ...)

    (p BAG3-ITEMS-IN-BAG ...)

    (p BAG4-ITEMS-IN-BAG ...)

    (p BAG5-ITEMS-IN-BAG ...)
```

These rules are used to put items in the specific bags.

```
11. (p LBAG-INITIALIZE-BAG-VECTOR ...)
    (p LBAG-INITIALIZE-ITEM-VECTOR ...)
    (p LBAG1 ...)
    (p LBAG2 ...)
    (p LBAG-QUAN1-CHECK ...)
    (p LBAG-QUAN2-CHECK ...)
    (p LBAG-QUAN3-CHECK ...)
    (p LBAG-QUAN4-CHECK ...)
    (p LBAG-LEAVE ...)
    (p LBAG-CHECK-TO-CONTINUE ...)
```

These rules deal with putting large items into a bag. The vectors have to be initialized, quantity limits have to be checked, the route has to be changed when the large items have all been bagged, and the search for large items has to be continued until all items have been checked.

```
12. (p MBAG-INITIALIZE-ITEM-VECTOR ...)
    (p MBAG-NEW-BAG ...)
    (p MBAG-CHECK-TO-CONTINUE ...)
    (p MBAG ...)
    (p MBAG-QUAN1-CHECK ...)
    (p MBAG-QUAN2-CHECK ...)
    (p MBAG-QUAN3-CHECK ...)
    (p MBAG-QUAN4-CHECK ...)
    (p MBAG-LEAVE-LAST-ITEM-M ...)
```

These rules deal with putting medium-sized items into a bag. The vectors have to be initialized, quantity limits have to be checked, the route has to be changed when the medium-sized items have all been bagged, and the search for items has to be continued until all items have been checked.

```
13. (p SBAG-INITIALIZE-BAG-VECTOR ...)
    (p SBAG-INITIALIZE-ITEM-VECTOR ...)
    (p SBAG-CHECK-TO-CONTINUE ...)
    (p SBAG ...)
```

```
(p SBAG-QUAN1-CHECK-TYPEL ...)
(p SBAG-QUAN1-CHECK-TYPEM ...)
(p SBAG-QUAN2-CHECK-TYPEL ...)
(p SBAG-QUAN2-CHECK-TYPEM ...)
(p SBAG-QUAN3-CHECK-TYPEL ...)
(p SBAG-QUAN3-CHECK-TYPEM ...)
(p SBAG-QUAN4-CHECK-TYPEL ...)
(p SBAG-QUAN4-CHECK-TYPEM ...)
(p SBAG1-LEAVE ...)
```

These rules deal with putting small items into bags that already have large and medium-sized items. The vectors have to be initialized, quantity limits have to be checked, the route has to be changed when the small items have all been bagged, and the search for small large items has to be continued until all items have been checked.

```
14. (p OUTPUT-ROUTINE-HEADER1 ...)
    (p OUTPUT-ROUTINE-HEADER2 ...)
    (p OUTPUT-ARRAY1-REROUT ...)
    (p OUTPUT-ARRAY2 ...)
    (p OUTPUT-ARRAY2-REROUT ...)
    (p OUTPUT-ARRAY3 ...)
    (p OUTPUT-ARRAY3-REROUT ...)
    (p OUTPUT-ARRAY4 ...)
    (p OUTPUT-ARRAY4-REROUT ...)
    (p OUTPUT-ARRAY5 ...)
    (p OUTPUT-ARRAY5-REROUT ...)
```

These rules deal with displaying the results of the bagging operation to the screen. They print out a header and then dump up to four bag arrays that contain the bagged items.

Example 8.3. Grocery bagging session

```
OPS5 > (load bagit.ops)
OPS5 > (make start)
OPS5 > (run)

---------------------------------------------
DATABASE FOR SYNTHESIS EXPERT SYSTEM BAG-IT

4/16/86   by P.Sherman

************* INITIAL CONDITIONS************
---------------------------------------------

CONTEXT LIST:

PEACHES......                MEDIUM      1
```

```
MILK.........            MEDIUM     3

APPLES.......            MEDIUM     1

COOKIES......            MEDIUM     2

HAMBURGER....            SMALL      2

BEER.........            LARGE      2

FROZ-WAFFLES.            SMALL      1

CHEESE.......            SMALL      3


BAG #  1          NUMBER OF ITEMS IN BAG  0          BAG FULL?  NO
...................................................................

ITEM              QUANTITY         FREEZER WRAPPED


0.....             0                 0




----------------------------------------------
DATABASE FOR SYNTHESIS EXPERT SYSTEM BAG-IT

************* FINISHED BAGGING *************
----------------------------------------------

BAG #  1          NUMBER OF ITEMS IN BAG  2          BAG FULL?  NO
...................................................................

ITEM              QUANTITY         FREEZER WRAPPED

BEER.........          2                 NO


BAG #  2          NUMBER OF ITEMS IN BAG  13          BAG FULL?  NO
...................................................................

ITEM              QUANTITY         FREEZER WRAPPED

PEACHES......          1                 NO
MILK.........          3                 NO
APPLES.......          1                 NO
```

```
COOKIES......          2                NO
HAMBURGER....          2                NO
FROZ-WAFFLES.          1                YES
CHEESE.......          3                NO
end -- no productions true
OPS5 >
```

8.3 REAL ESTATE MATCHING

This case study analyses real estate listings (parcels of land for sale) and matches them to the needs of prospective commercial developers. The listings are represented in a data file like the one in Example 8.4. The file contains information about the size of the lot, the location, zoning (number of stories), multi-story expansion potential, and the cost. The prospective buyer is asked how much office space will be needed and how many employees will be working at the office.

This project is presented as a software engineering exercise and the whole design is documented as a software project would be. Example 8.5 shows a planning document typical of the initial phase of such a project. Example 8.6 represents the requirement specifications of the project. Example 8.7 represents the design document of the project. The disk accompanying this book contains the complete source code for this example in the file `EXARCH.OPS`. Example 8.8 shows the program running.

Example 8.4. Real estate data

```
file.p

index   # of items
0        25

size      location   # of stories    flag      cost
100000      city          ms          no      850000
50000       sub           ms          no      250000
30000       city          ms          no      250000
75000       sub           ss          no      300000
20000       sub           ss          no      100000
stop
```

Example 8.5. Project plan

TO: Dr. Apte, Vice President of R and D
FROM: Porter Sherman, Expert System Project Leader
SUBJECT: Plan for a Commercial Real Estate Planning System
DATE: 4/14/86

I. SCOPE OF SYSTEM

This system will be designed to access current real estate listings as they exist in a computer database. The program will query the user as to the requirements and it will match the input requirements to existing real estate offerings. The system will be able to repeat the matching for as long as the user wants to continue specifying new requirements. The user will be asked two things: the total square feet needed and the estimated number of employees that will work at the building.

The system will make decisions based on zoning restrictions related to each real estate parcel in the listing. The output from the system will identify each parcel that fits the requirements. Each matched parcel will also have pertinent information included: cost of the parcel, location, zoning, number of stories required, and the building cost estimate (this is related to the current building costs and will have to be updated continuously).

II. TASKS AND DELIVERABLES

A. Tasks

1. Requirements Analysis
2. Design
3. Unit Coding
4. Integration Test

B. Deliverables

1. Plan
2. Requirements Specification
3. Design Document
4. Program Listing
5. Future Considerations

III. RESOURCES

A. One Graduate Student

B. One IBM-AT

IV. COST

30 hours/person x 20.00 dollars/hour = 30 x 20.00 = 600.00
10 hours/person x 75.00 dollars/hour = 10 x 75.00 = 750.00
Total = 1350.00

V. SCHEDULE

Week of 4/14	Two hours for developing the plan Five hours for developing the requirement specification
Week of 4/21	Seven hours for developing the design and design document
Week of 4/28	Four hours for coding on computer Two hours for developing test procedures
Week of 5/5	Six hours for integration testing on computer
Week of 5/12	Four hours for future considerations and presentation

Example 8.6. Requirements

TO: Dr. Apte, Vice President of R and D
FROM: Porter Sherman, Expert System Project Leader
SUBJECT: Requirement Specification
DATE: 4/21/86

I. SCOPE AND OBJECTIVE

The main objective is to access a real estate database and to match listings with building needs in accordance with the guidelines in Part I of the planning document.

II. PROCESS DESCRIPTION

A. INITIALIZE AND INPUT

1. INITIALIZE:

(a) Set up all items to be processed as variables or arrays such as routing, requirements, listing, solution set, temporary holding, flags, and optimizing pre-evaluations.

2. INPUT:

(a) Open and read into an array the current real estate listing file. This is limited to 128 items because of the limits of the machine being used.
(b) Prompt the user to enter the desired number of square feet needed for building and the number of employees to be hired. Input these into the requirement variables.

B. MATCH REQUIREMENTS TO LISTINGS

1. MULTIPLE-STORY ZONE

(a) Any listing that is zoned for multiple stories is identified as valid. This gives the builder the option to add stories to get the required footage.

2. SINGLE-STORY ZONE

(a) Any requirement that is greater than the listing is declared not valid since there is no option to add stories to gain the needed footage.
(b) Any requirement that is less than the listing must be equated with the qualifier of city or suburb. The reason behind this is that the parking situation must be considered where city development will rely on mass transit and suburb development will have most employees driving to work.

C. CONFIGURE THE SELECTED LISTINGS

1. SINGLE-STORY BUILDING

Any listing that is sufficiently larger than the requirements so that it will allow adequate parking for employees is designated single story. Two different configurations are used: one for city and one for suburb because of different building costs and parking restrictions.

2. TWO-STORY BUILDING

(Note: This is checked only if the one-story test failed.) Any listing that is larger than one half the required space such that it will allow adequate parking for employees is designated two story. Two different configurations are used: one for city and one for suburb because of different building costs and parking restrictions.

3. THREE-STORY BUILDING

(Note: This is checked only if the two-story test failed.) Any listing that is larger than one third the required space such that it will allow adequate parking for employees is designated three story. Two different configurations are used: one for city and one for suburb because of different building costs and parking restrictions.

4. FOUR-STORY BUILDING

(Note: This is checked only if the three-story test failed.) Any listing that is larger than one fourth the required space such that it will allow adequate parking for employees is designated four story. Two different configurations are used: one for city and one for suburb because of different building costs and parking restrictions.

D. OUTPUT AND RUN AGAIN OPTION

1. OUTPUT

A configured list of all valid real estate offerings is presented after the program has checked every listing that was input from the listing file.

2. RUN AGAIN OPTION

The user can opt to run the program again where the listing file is input again and the user is prompted to enter new requirements. Otherwise, the program will end.

III. DESCRIPTION OF SYSTEM OPERATION

This system is designed to access an existing database and to allow limited user interaction. The initial setup of the system will be the opening of a known file and loading an array with the data from that file. This data will represent current real estate offerings. Then the user will be asked to enter two building requirements:

(a) Total number of square feet that are required for his building.

(b) Total number of employees that will be working at the building.

With this information the system will determine which of the current listings (if any) are adequate for the user's requirements. The first thing that is done is a size matching in relation to zoning restrictions. This determines if the listing is valid for configuration to the user's requirements. When all valid listings are identified, then the system will configure each listing to the user's needs and it will develop a cost estimate of the whole package. A complete list of each configuration is printed out to the screen for the user to see. At the end of the session the user is asked if he wants to run the system again.

IV. TESTING: BOTTOM UP

The approach to testing will be modular. Each process is a separate module and has a specific routing qualifier in the LHS of the process rules. Thus by setting up dummy instantiations each process can be tested separately for correctness. Once each process is working satisfactorily, then they can be integrated into a full system. (Note: specific language syntax for operations such as arrays and files was proven in small test programs external to the processes themselves.)

Final testing with the user will be handled in the time allowed, but it must be stated that future maintenance will be needed, as operation bugs are sure to arise as system use increases.

Example 8.7. Design Document

TO: Dr. Apte, Vice President of R and D
FROM: Porter Sherman, Expert System Project Leader
SUBJECT: Commercial Real Estate Planning System Design Document
DATE: 5/5/86

DESIGN DOCUMENT

CONTENTS

SECTION I	IDENTIFICATION AND SCOPE
SECTION II	BIBLIOGRAPHY
SECTION III	DESIGN LANGUAGE
SECTION IV	FLOW OF CONTROL
SECTION V	DATA STRUCTURE
SECTION VI	ACCEPTANCE CRITERIA
SECTION VII	LIMITATIONS

SECTION I IDENTIFICATION AND SCOPE

The main objective is to simulate the decision process that an expert in real estate planning would have to go through according to the guidelines in PART I of the Planning Document.

SECTION II BIBLIOGRAPHY

PLANNING DOCUMENT APRIL 14,1986

REQUIREMENT SPECIFICATIONS APRIL 21,1986

SECTION III DESIGN LANGUAGE

The design language that will be used is the OPS5 Expert System design language. This is a rule-based production system language that has forward chaining built into its inference engine.

SECTION IV FLOW OF CONTROL

1. INITIALIZE FUNCTION

```
MAKE all variables initial conditions
OPEN real estate file
FOR ALL ITEMS in the file
        LOAD each item into the listing array
PRINT explanation heading
QUERY user for input
INPUT FROM TERMINAL the two requirements and store in variables
EVALUATE any equations that can be evaluated
```

2. VALIDATION FUNCTION

```
FILL TEMP VARIABLES with one listing from listing array
MATCH temp variables with appropriate valid/not valid rule
IF all items from listing array are done
THEN route to configure
ELSE goto FILL TEMP VARIABLES
```

3. CONFIGURE FUNCTION

```
FILL TEMP VARIABLES with valid listing from listing array
MATCH temp variables with appropriate story configuration and cost estimate.
IF all items from listing array are done
   THEN route to output
   ELSE goto FILL TEMP VARIABLES
```

4. OUTPUT FUNCTION

```
PRINT explanation heading
FOR EACH VALID LISTING
   PRINT configured list
QUERY if user wants run again
   INPUT FROM TERMINAL yes or no
   IF YES route to initialize
```

SECTION V DATA STRUCTURE

1. VARIABLES

```
(a) requirements ^rsqft = number of square feet needed
                 ^remploy = number of employees

(b) rout ^rvalue = process to be performed
                 = any of these names:
                   valid-parcels
                   configure
                   output
                   load-temp-parcel

(c) evaluations  ^sub-cars = 80% of the employees will drive in suburb
                           = (.80 * ^remploy)*60
                 ^city-cars = 60% of the employees will drive in city
                           = (.40 * ^remploy)*60
```

(d) temp-parcel ^tsqfeet = square feet in listing
^tloc = city or suburb
^tzone = single or multiple story
^tvalid = yes or no
^tcost = price of listing

(e) iterate-flag ^iterate = yes or no to iterate in the fill-temp rule

(f) heading ^printed = yes or no that the explanation heading was printed already

(g) loop-count ^count = index of how many times we have gone through loop

2. ARRAYS

(a) parcels ^pindex = points to the location of the next listing in the parray

^pend = points to end of the parray
^parray = listing array
loc1 = number of square feet in the listing
loc2 = city or suburb
loc3 = single or multiple story
loc4 = valid: yes or no
loc5 = price of listing

(b) solution ^sindex = points to the location of the next valid, configured listing in the sarray

^send = points to end of the sarray

^sarray = valid,configured listings
loc1 = price of listing
loc2 = required square feet
loc3 = number of employees
loc4 = square feet in listing
loc5 = city or suburb
loc6 = number of stories needed
loc7 = building cost estimate

(c) routing ˆrindex = points to the location of the next route in the rarray
ˆrarray = array of process routes
loc1 = valid-parcels
loc2 = configure
loc3 = output

3. CONSTANTS

(a) Building cost per story
1. city = $150,000
2. suburb = $100,000
(b) Parking lot cost
$1,000 per car

SECTION VI ACCEPTANCE CRITERIA

In order for the system to be accepted, it must perform according to the criteria stated in PART III of the Requirement Specification Document.

SECTION VII LIMITATIONS

There is a limit of 128 items that can be stored in an array when using a PC-based OPS5 language. All other limitations are those set down in PART I of the Planning Document of April 14, 1986 and in PART IV of the Requirements Specification Document of April 21, 1986.

TO: Dr. Apte, Vice President of R and D
FROM: Porter Sherman, Expert System Project Leader
SUBJECT: Commercial Real Estate Planning System
Future Considerations
DATE: 5/14/86

FUTURE CONSIDERATIONS

The Commercial Real Estate Planning System is a simulation of a task that is generally performed by experts in real estate planning. The scope of the program was intentionally limited so that certain concepts could be proven. These concepts were:

(a) That a real estate database can be accessed.
(b) That requirements can be matched to existing offerings in relation to specific qualifiers.
(c) That composite evaluations can be derived.

(d) That a user-friendly format can be obtained.

The next step will be to have an expert evaluate the program and add to it. Facilities to explain how configurations were derived are also needed, as well as a maintenance program so that changes in the values of the constants can be accommodated.

Another consideration would be to add a section to actually design the building. This could entail taking an existing design from a database and embellishing it or interfacing to a CAD program and designing from scratch. An expert system can be built to spec out all the building material requirements associated with the design. Depending on the extent of the database, the system might come up with a few different scenarios of building design.

The data structure set up for this program is as follows:

1. The record to hold the values of the square feet required and number of employees.

CLASS	ATTRIBUTES
requirements	rsqft
	remploy

2. The records to hold the arrays of values of the listing of parcel information and the solution information.

CLASS	ATTRIBUTES
parcels	pindex
	pend
	parray
solution	sindex
	send
	sarray

3. The record to hold the values of the evaluations that determine the parking lot requirements.

CLASS	ATTRIBUTES
evaluations	sub-cars
	city-cars
N-n	
	N-nd2
	N-nd3
	N-nd4

4. The records to hold the values of the routing variables.

CLASS	ATTRIBUTES
routing	rindex
	rarray
rout	rvalue

5. The records to hold the values of flags, loop indexes, and temporary information.

CLASS	ATTRIBUTES
temp-parcel	tsqfeet
	tloc
	tzone
	tvalid
	tcost
iterate-flag	iterate
header	printed
loop-count	count
file-count	fcnt
	floop

The rules used in this program are described as follows:

1. `(p INIT ...)`

This rule prints the header out to the screen, questions the user for information, and loads WM with all the initial data.

2.
```
(p FILL-PARCEL-INDEX-FROM-FILE ...)
(p FILL-PARCEL-VECTOR-FROM-FILE ...)
(p CLOSE-PARCEL-FILE ...)
```

These rules handle the opening of the file that has the listing, in this case file.p, load the parcels array with the data, and close the file.

3.
```
(p VALID-CHECK-INITIAL ...)
(p VALID-CHECK-MULTI-STORY-ZONE ...)
(p VALID-CHECK-SINGLE-STORY-ZONE-PAR-REQ ...)
(p VALID-CHECK-SINGLE-STORY-ZONE-SUB ...)
(p VALID-CHECK-SINGLE-STORY-ZONE-CITY ...)
(p VALID-CHECK-TO-CONTINUE ...)
(p VALID-CHECK-FINISHED...)
```

These rules check through the parcel listing and determine which parcels can be configured to the requirements of the user.

4. (p CONFIGURE-INITIAL ...)
   (p CONFIGURE-ONE-STORY-SUBURB ...)
   (p CONFIGURE-ONE-STORY-CITY ...)
   (p CONFIGURE-TWO-STORY-SUBURB ...)
   (p CONFIGURE-TWO-STORY-CITY ...)
   (p CONFIGURE-THREE-STORY-SUBURB ...)
   (p CONFIGURE-THREE-STORY-CITY ...)
   (p CONFIGURE-FOUR-STORY-SUBURB ...)
   (p CONFIGURE-FOUR-STORY-CITY ...)
   (p VALID-CONFIGURE-TO-CONTINUE ...)
   (p NOT-VALID-CONFIGURE-TO-CONTINUE ...)
   (p CONFIGURE-FINISHED ...)

These rules perform the configurations of the parcels to the required specifications of the user. Different configurations are based on zone laws that determine parking space and number of stories.

5. (p OUTPUT-MATCHED-PARCELS-INITIAL ...)
   (p OUTPUT-MATCHED-PARCELS-MAIN-DRIVER ...)
   (p OUTPUT-MATCHED-PARCELS-FINISHED ...)

These rules will print out to the screen the results of the configurations.

6. (p RESTART-QUERY ...)
   (p RESTART-YES ...)

These rules determine if the user wants to run the program again.

7. (p FILL-TEMP-PARCEL ...)
   (p FILL-TEMP-PARCEL-CATCH-ALL ...)

These rules are used to store temporary data in WM.

Example 8.8. Running the real estate system

```
OPS5 > (load exarch.ops)
OPS5 > (make start)
OPS5 > (run)

*******************************************************************
                  REAL ESTATE CONFIGURATION SYSTEM

This program is designed to take projected building requirements and
match them to existing real estate offerings.

Input restrictions: (1) size of building in square feet
                    (2) number of employees that will work there
                    (3) database is undeveloped parcels of land

*** Please enter the answers to the following questions:

1. How much office area (in square feet) do you need ?  10000
```

```
2. How many employees will be working in the office ?  50

*** The program is matching your requirements to a parcel...

******************************************************************

THE FOLLOWING IS A BREAKDOWN OF AVAILABLE REAL ESTATE MATCHED TO THESE
BUILDING REQUIREMENTS:

SQUARE FEET REQUIRED =  10000     NUMBER OF EMPLOYEES =  50

BUILDING COST ESTIMATE IS EVALUATED FOR EACH PARCEL
----------------------------------------------------------------

PARCEL NUMBER <CNT>     PARCEL COST = $850000

TOTAL SQUARE FEET =  100000     STORIES NEEDED =  ONE-STORY

ESTIMATED BUILDING COST = $1020000     LOCATION:  CITY

----------------------------------------------------------------

PARCEL NUMBER <CNT>     PARCEL COST = $250000

TOTAL SQUARE FEET =  50000      STORIES NEEDED =  ONE-STORY

ESTIMATED BUILDING COST = $390000      LOCATION:  SUB

----------------------------------------------------------------

PARCEL NUMBER <CNT>     PARCEL COST = $250000

TOTAL SQUARE FEET =  30000      STORIES NEEDED =  ONE-STORY

ESTIMATED BUILDING COST = $420000      LOCATION:  CITY

----------------------------------------------------------------

PARCEL NUMBER <CNT>     PARCEL COST = $300000

TOTAL SQUARE FEET =  75000      STORIES NEEDED =  ONE-STORY

ESTIMATED BUILDING COST = $440000      LOCATION:  SUB

----------------------------------------------------------------

PARCEL NUMBER <CNT>     PARCEL COST = $100000
```

```
TOTAL SQUARE FEET =  20000      STORIES NEEDED =  ONE-STORY

ESTIMATED BUILDING COST = $240000      LOCATION:  SUB

.......................................................

***** ANOTHER SET OF BUILDING REQUIREMENTS ?
PLEASE ENTER Y or N ......  n

 end -- no productions true
OPS5 >
```

8.4 SUMMARY

These case studies demonstrate how OPS5 can be used to encapsulate expertise and solve problems. The input and output operations in OPS5 are limited and it is recommended that the interface be built in another language if need be. Also note how complicated array operations can be. These cases are presented as examples of what can be done with OPS5. The reader should spend the time required to become familiar with the OPS5 operations in these cases. It would be advisable to try to change some of the rules or add new rules and see what side effects occur. This will give the reader a true sense of what it is like to maintain an existing system. The next step, after the reader has mastered these simple systems, is to design a system from planning document through working code.

9

THE NEXT GENERATION: OPS83

9.1 OVERVIEW

OPS5 has been successfully used for many expert systems, yet there are situations where it cannot be easily used. In our own work, we have seen expert systems that were not adopted because they could not be delivered economically or could not integrate with existing systems. While OPS5 requires less resources than some other large expert system environments, it would still not be possible to deliver an OPS5 system with thousands of rules on an IBM PC.

The creator of OPS5, Charles L. Forgy, has written a new language, OPS83, to succeed OPS5. While OPS5 has been used for things such as research in Artificial Intelligence and Cognitive Psychology, OPS83 was designed expressly as an expert systems programming language. It has a more complex syntax than OPS5, but is one of the most efficient and flexible rule-based languages available. OPS83 is largely written in C, and this has three implications. First, OPS83 is available on a wide variety of machines, from small IBM PC-compatible machines to most popular workstations and the largest VAX computers. Therefore, one can deliver in any of these environments and quickly port to another machine with no modification of source code. Second, OPS83 is very efficient. Benchmarks of programs can be very misleading, so we will not quote runtimes or rules fired per second here, but OPS83 programs can be many times faster than their OPS5 counterparts, and the executable programs are always much smaller. Third, OPS83 programs can easily call external routines written in C, so interfacing with graphics packages and databases is much more efficient and convenient than it is in most versions of OPS5.

A problem with OPS5 is that it requires everything to be done using rules, even when other forms of control would be easier. For example, there are times when a FOR loop is the most natural way to express part of an algorithm. As we have shown earlier, it is possible to emulate FOR loops in OPS5, but the code is not as natural as it would be if there were an actual FOR construct. OPS83 not only allows FOR loops, but also WHILE loops, procedures, and function calls. In fact, one can write OPS83 programs that have no rules at all and look similar to programs written in C or Pascal. The real strength of OPS83 is that it allows one to go back and forth between the rule-based style of programming, and traditional, *imperative programming*-style programming.

Most versions of OPS5 are interpreted, while OPS83 is a compiled language. Interpreters are typically characterized by slower execution speeds, but often allow easier debugging of programs. With an OPS5 interpreter, one can interactively type declarations and rules, and modify or examine working memory. An OPS83 program, on the other hand, is kept in a file or files that are compiled, linked with other code, and run. The resulting program can be fairly small, since there is not an entire interpreter needed as with OPS5.

We cannot teach all there is to know about OPS83 in one chapter, but we can compare OPS83 and OPS5 in terms of syntax, flexibility, performance, and cost.

9.2 DATA STRUCTURES

Remember that OPS5 supports only one type of basic data structure, the working memory element. Elements have values that are numbers or symbols, but values are not assigned a fixed type. This means that if one declares a working memory element with: `(literalize automobile color cost)`, one can legally put any value in any attribute, such as: `(make automobile ^color 5600 ^cost red)` even though that is likely to be an error. In other programming languages, it is common to declare the type of a data structure, so, for example, one might restrict `cost` to being only numbers, and `color` to being only a string, or even just a member of a certain set of colors. OPS83, like most programming languages, requires data structures to have declared types. On the one hand, this makes things less flexible, but it also means that many semantic errors will be caught by the OPS83 compiler. No doubt it also helps the efficiency of OPS83.

The primitive data types of OPS83 are integer, real, logical, character, and symbol. These types can also be components of more complicated types, such as arrays, records, and working memory elements. There is also the idea of derived types, which is a concept present in Pascal and (to some extent) in C. Derived types allow new types to be declared that inherit the properties of an existing type. Any variable then declared with a derived type can only be used with other variables of the same type, thus allowing the compiler to catch semantic errors that might pass through in another language.

One can convert between some types by using the `cast` statement. For example, one might want to convert an integer value to a real. Casting is a common operation in languages such as C, and a common cause of strange behavior in C programs is forgetting to cast a variable or constant to the type that a function expects. OPS83 is much more strict about casting variables, and will not allow programs to compile without the proper casts. This is either good or bad, depending on the programmer's outlook.

All variables in OPS83 must be declared before they are used, and declarations come in three forms: global variables, local variables, and parameters to functions and procedures. Here are some example global variable declarations:

```
global
     &Age : integer,
     &Speed : real,
     &Antique : logical,
     &C : character,
     &Brand : symbol;
```

This declares one variable from each of the five primitive classes. There are two interesting things about the syntax. The first is that variables always begin with the ampersand character (&), and the second is that the declarations are separated by commas, and the whole thing is ended with a semi-colon. A variable declared globally will be accessible by any rule, function, or procedure within the module that it is declared in (modules will be defined in a later section, but for now, think of a module as a file). A variable can also be declared locally using the keyword `local`, which means that it will be usable only in the rule, function, or procedure where it is declared. Local variables are created each time a rule, function, or procedure is invoked, and do not retain their values between invocations. Declarations of variables for functions and procedures will be covered in a following section.

One of the most awkward features of OPS5 is the use of vectors. Vectors in OPS5 are much like one-dimensional arrays in other languages. However, OPS5 requires that there be no more than one vector per working memory element, and that it be the last attribute in the element. Getting data in and out of vectors is not as easy as in other languages either, as we have seen in an earlier chapter. OPS83 allows users to declare arrays of variables, and arrays can more easily be part of working memory elements. Array indices begin at 1 rather than at 0 as in C. Like C and Pascal, multi-dimensional arrays can be declared, although the syntax is not intuitive. In the following example, we declare a one-dimensional array and a two-dimensional array:

```
global &BattingAverages : array(25:real),     -- a one dimensional array
       &Scores : array(9: array(2:integer)); -- a two dimensional array
```

The first element of the first array is called `&BattingAverages[1]`, and the last is called `&BattingAverages[25]`. To find the score of the second team in the fourth inning of a game, one would look at `&Scores[4][2]`.

Like C and Pascal, OPS83 allows declaration of records. Records are very similar in structure to working memory elements in that they have named fields containing values of different types. Records differ from working memory elements in that they can be passed as arguments to functions and procedures, since they are variables, they can also be referred to by name.

Here is a declaration of a record type called `BaseballPlayer`, and its use by an array called `&Team`.

```
type BaseballPlayer = record
(name : symbol;
 HomeRuns : integer;
 GamesPlayed : integer;
 YearsWithTeam : real;
);

local
   &Team : array(25:BaseballPlayer);
```

If player number 12 hit a home run, we could update his score with the statement

```
&Team[12].HomeRuns = &Team[12].HomeRuns + 1;
```

Another important feature in OPS83 is the ability to use derived types. Derived types are a way of telling the compiler some extra information about the meanings of variables, so that it can help catch semantic errors at compile time. Suppose, for example, we had an OPS83 function that computed the batting average of a player:

```
function battingAvg(&hits : integer, &atBat : integer) : real
  {
    if (&atBat = 0)
       return (0.0)
    else return(&hits/&atBat);
  };
```

Suppose the programmer called `battingAvg` in the following way:

```
for &I = (1 to 25)
   {
      &P[&i].average = battingAvg(&P[&I].hits, &P[&I].atBat);
   };
```

It would be quite easy to transpose the two arguments to the function accidentally, such as

```
for &I = (1 to 25)
   {
      &P[&i].average = battingAvg(&P[&I].atBat, &P[&I].hits);
   };
```

This code would compile correctly, and even run without error, although the player's batting averages would end up incorrect if he had any hits. With good use of derived types, we would allow the compiler to catch errors such as this one. For example, we could declare things like this:

```
type timesAtBat = integer;
type numberOfHits = integer;
type BAvg = real;

type player = record
  (
    hits : numberOfHits;
    atBat : timesAtBat;
    average : BAvg;
  );

P : array(25 : player);

function battingAvg(&hits : numberOfHits, &atBat : timesAtBat) : BAvg
 {
    if (&atBat = 0)
        return (0.0)
    else return(&hits/&atBat);
  };

for &I = (1 to 25)
   {
      &P[&i].average = battingAvg(&P[&I].hits, &P[&I].atBat);
   };
```

The `type timesAtBat = integer;` creates a new type which can handle the same operations as integers, but which is a bit more restrictive in terms of assignment and parameter passing. Now, if the programmer made the same mistake as before, the compiler would warn about the type clash.

9.3 WORKING MEMORY

In the preceding section, we talked about declaring variables. Declaring a variable means choosing a name and specifying its type. The compiler then allocates the proper amount of storage for that variable. Declaring working memory is somewhat similar to declaring variables, but with working memory, we are declaring the *kinds* of elements that can appear, not specifying the number of them, or giving them names. Thus, an OPS83 compiler does not allocate space for working memory elements in advance, and we can make, modify, or remove them at will in our program, as long as we specify the correct types of data.

A typical working memory element declaration might be

```
type automobile = element
  (
    maker : symbol;
    model : symbol;
    weight : integer;
    milesPerGallon : real;
    age : integer;
  );
```

After this declaration, all of the following would be legal ways to place a new automobile working memory element in working memory:

```
make (automobile maker=ford; model=pinto; weight=2200);
make (automobile maker=porsche; age=1);
make (automobile maker=vw; model=bug; weight=1700; milesPerGallon=35; age=20);
```

Values that are not explicitly set when the element is made are set to a reasonable default depending on the type.

9.4 RULES

The overall structure of an OPS83 rule is roughly the same as an OPS5 rule, but the details of the syntax are almost completely different. Much of the syntax of OPS5 comes from the fact that it was originally written in LISP. This accounts for the many parentheses and for the choice of semi-colon as a comment character. Incidentally, in OPS83, the two-character sequence `--` (two minus signs) is used to begin comments. Therefore, everything on a line following two minus signs is ignored. It should not need to be said that code should be commented liberally for the benefit of others and for yourself in the future. As in all languages, comments can be overdone. If you have chosen an obvious name for a variable, the name is self-commenting, and nothing further is needed. All too often, code contains lines such as

```
&TotalHits : integer;   -- This variable contains the total hits
```

In OPS83, a rule to delete all Fords from working memory would look like this:

```
rule removeFords
{
    &1 (goal maker=ford);
-->
      remove &1;
};
```

Notice the keyword **rule**, which takes the place of **(p** in OPS5. The name of the rule follows, as in OPS83, and then the body of the rule is enclosed in curly brackets, and terminated with a semi-colon. The differences between OPS5 rules and OPS83 rules run deeper, however. One can include certain types of function calls in the patterns on the left-hand sides of rules, and one can have very general code (such as the types discussed in the next section) on the right-hand sides of rules.

9.5 CONTROL STRUCTURES

Perhaps the most important difference between OPS5 and OPS83 is the availability of imperative programming constructs such as **for**, **while**, and **if**. While some complex tasks are efficiently expressed in OPS5, there are also some very simple tasks that are awkward to express. For example, in OPS5, printing the numbers 1 to 100 in order requires 100 recognize-select-act cycles, and involves creating some additional working memory elements that do not serve a very interesting purpose. If the interpreter averaged 10 rules per second, we have wasted 10 seconds doing something that is easy in many simpler languages. Fortunately, OPS83 provides a **for** construct for things that can make use of it.

```
for &I = (1 to 10)
    write() |I am |, &I, | years old now.|, '\\n';
```

The syntax for the **while** loop is easy to guess. Remember that the condition must be of type logical.

```
while (&needMore)
   {
      read() &X;
      process(&X);
   };
```

True and *false* in OPS83 are represented as **1b** and **0b**, respectively, so an endless loop could be expressed as follows:

```
while (1b)
{
    write () |I will not raise taxes.|;
};
```

There is also an **if** (and **if else**) statement in OPS83. The syntax is straightforward:

```
if (&Age > 18 /\ &Age < 65)
    write () |Your ticket costs $5.00|
else write () |Your ticket costs $2.00|;
```

9.6 FUNCTIONS AND PROCEDURES

It would be unthinkable to program in Pascal or C without functions and procedures. They allow us to put code in one place and call it from many places, avoiding repetition. It also allows us to debug programs a piece at a time, often localizing errors to a specific block of code. An example of a procedure in OPS83 is

```
procedure count(&N : integer)
{
  local &I : integer;

  for &I = (1 to &N)
      write() &I, ' ';
}
```

As in Pascal, procedures are declared with the keyword `procedure`, followed by a procedure name and parameters enclosed in parentheses. The syntax of the parameter declarations is also similar to Pascal, but of course variable names begin with ampersands.

Functions and procedures can be *simple* or *non-simple*. In OPS83, *simple* means "free of side effects," and hence usable in the left-hand side of a rule. Side effects include `read`, `write`, `make`, `modify`, and `remove` statements. If a function had side effects such as these, irreversible things would happen during the pattern match phase of the recognize-act cycle, even if the rule did not fire. We really want actions to be on the right-hand side of rules, so that they execute only when a rule fires. An example of a simple function is

```
simple function d(&x1:integer,&y1:integer,&x2:integer,&y2:integer):integer
{
   return(sqrt(&x1*&x2+3*&y1*&y2));
}
```

Recursive functions and procedures are allowed in OPS83, and there is even a way to have recursive recognize-act cycles, so that there can be hierarchies of rules running.

9.7 USING MODULES

Regardless of the programming language, good software engineering dictates modular programs when a program becomes large. At the lower level, a program should be broken into functions and procedures, and at a higher level, large amounts of code should be placed in multiple files or modules. A significant feature of OPS83 over OPS5 is that it supports modules.

The benefits of modules are many: First, multiple programmers can each work on modules independently, with the results integrated later. Second, the amount of code to be compiled when small changes are made is often small. Of course, some changes to a program will require all modules to be recompiled, but in general, this will save a large amount of time. Third, once a module is reasonably well debugged, it can almost be eliminated from consideration when tracking down new errors.

Like many good things, there is a cost to using modules, and that is that they require a bit of planning initially. Related procedures, functions, and rules should of course go in a common module, with only a small number of each being called from other modules. If a project is big enough to require modules, it might be wise to draw a block diagram showing the modules and their interconnections before writing much code.

Let us imagine that we have a program composed of three modules: *parser*, *diagnoser*, and *explainer*. The first procedure to execute will be in the module *diagnoser*.

The code in the parser file will look like this:

```
module parser()
{
 use diagnoser;

 -- parser procedures here

}
```

The code in the diagnoser file will look like this:

```
module diagnoser(start)
{
 use parser, explainer;

 -- diagnoser procedures here

 procedure start() {
 -- body of start here
 };
}
```

The code in the explainer file will look like this:

```
module explainer()
{
 use diagnoser;

 -- explainer procedures here

}
```

In this scenario, `parser` and `explainer` should be compiled before `diagnoser`, and `diagnoser` must be recompiled each time that one of the others is recompiled.

9.8 CUSTOMIZING THINGS

In previous chapters, we saw that OPS5 has a very well defined way of doing things. Rules are matched against working memory, conflict resolution happens using either the LEX or MEA strategy, and one rule is then fired. Any set of rules that runs in one OPS5 interpreter will run the same way in any other. This is an advantage in some ways, but is less flexible. OPS83 does not enforce any particular conflict resolution strategy, but instead has functions and procedures that can be used to write a conflict resolution strategy. Thus, one can implement LEX or MEA-like strategies, or make up completely different ones. Rules can even have *rates*, which are weights between 0 and 1. The conflict resolution strategy can use the rates to give preference to some rules over others. One can probe for information about partially matched rules.

The calls that enable one to write a custom conflict resolution procedure are: `cssize()`, `instance()`, and `fire`. Two of them, `cssize()` and `fire`, are quite simple and intuitive. The first simply returns the number of instantiations currently in the conflict set. The second accepts an integer between 1 and the value returned by `cssize()`, and fires that rule with its matching data. In between these two calls, we must select which instantiation dominates by using the `instance()` function. It is not worth discussing in complete detail here, but it accepts an integer corresponding to a specific instantiation, and returns information such as the number of working memory elements that are involved, the number of patterns on the left-hand side of the rule, the number of times that this instantiation has been used previously, and so on.

In order to write a conflict resolution procedure, one would typically use the following structure:

```
&ruleToFire = 0;
for &x = (1 to cssize())
   -- call instance on each instantiation, and keep track of the
   -- most likely rule to fire in &ruleToFire
fire &ruleToFire;
```

At first the compiled nature of OPS83 makes it seem like a very difficult environment to debug in. In the simplest OPS83 program, one calls the run procedure, the program runs, and then exits. If something went wrong, one cannot look at working memory after the fact to see what it contains (as is possible in OPS5). Fortunately, one can write an interactive top level in OPS83 itself, and link it with any program. One such top level comes with OPS83, and can be modified any way the programmer chooses. When the top level is linked to an OPS83 program, one first goes to a command interpreter which allows modification or examination of working memory, changing of trace information, and beginning the recognize-act cycle.

9.9 COMPILATION AND LINKING

The topic of compiling and linking OPS83 programs is difficult to explain in detail, since it is machine dependent, but we will give several examples. Since it is compiled rather than interpreted like OPS5, the procedure for running an OPS83 program is substantially different.

First of all, if your system provides a program building facility like the UNIX `make` program, by all means use it. Debugging an OPS83 program will take some iterations of editing and compiling, and repeatedly typing these commands will be tedious without a tool to help.

There are two binary files that come with OPS83 that must always be linked in with the code that you write in order to build a working program. They are called `crts83.o` and `mrts83.o`. Suppose we have an OPS83 program in one file called `prog.ops`. We invoke the OPS83 compiler on this file with the command: `ops83 prog.ops`. We will see a message something like this:

```
OPS83 ver. 2.2C.  Copyright (C) 1983 Production Systems Technologies, Inc.
```

This message is followed by any error messages that the compiler produces. If there are error messages, one must edit the file `prog.ops` again until no errors remain. After the file compiles error free, you will notice a file `prog.s` in the directory. This file must run through the assembler on the system. On a UNIX system, this step looks like: `as prog.s -o prog.o`. It is highly unlikely that there will be any errors during this phase. Now the directory will contain the file `prog.o`. This must be linked with `crts83.o` and `mrts83.o` using the C compiler. Under UNIX, this looks like: `cc prog.o crts83.o mrts83.o -o prog`. Now the executable file `prog` can be run by typing its name. It is reasonable to delete the files ending with `.s` after they are used, but it is better to save `.o` files during development, since they are often linked with other `.o` files, and with the use of a `make` facility, you can use the `.o` files corresponding to `.c` files that have not changed. Be particularly careful not to type a command to remove all `.o` files at once (such as `rm *.o` in UNIX), because you will delete the `crts83.o` and `mrts83.o` files if they are in the same directory as your OPS83 code. In general, compiling and assembling an OPS83 program is extremely fast. However, the linking of the code takes varying amounts of time, depending on the C compiler of the target machine. For serious development efforts, you will want to develop on a workstation rather than a small PC when possible. Since the code is quite portable, you can easily compile the final code on any machine that runs OPS83 with no modification.

9.10 EXTERNAL CALLS

Since OPS83 is a fairly rich programming language, it will not often be necessary to "escape" to another programming language in order to express something that cannot be done in OPS83. However, some people might like to talk to an existing database, to control a robotic arm, to use a graphics package, or to communicate with another program. OPS83 allows external calls to be made for this reason. The other programming language must adhere to some guidelines in order to be compatible. First, it must be able to accept variables passed by reference (rather than by value). Second, it must follow the same linkage conventions as C on the target machine. Third, it must use the same data representations as OPS83.

The safest bet for external code that must be written is C, since OPS83 itself is written in C, and is similar with respect to the conventions above. We will present a short example of calling an external graphics package from OPS83. Suppose our graphics package is written in C, and contains the following primitives:

- `clearScreen();`
- `drawLine(color, x1, y1, x2, y2);`
- `drawCircle(color, x, y, r);`

In our OPS83 program, we must declare the three procedures as follows:

```
external procedure clearScreen();
external procedure drawLine(&C, &X1, &Y1, &X2, &Y2 : out integer);
external procedure drawCircle(&C, &X, &Y, &R : out integer);
```

Our OPS83 program would then use these drawing primitives as follows:

```
procedure drawBarbell()
{
  LOCAL
    &height : integer;
    &width : integer;

  write() |height ? |;
  read() &height;
  write() |width ? |;
  read() &width;

  call clearScreen();
  call drawLine(1, 10, &height, 10 + &width, &height);
  call drawCircle(1, 10, &height, &height);
  call drawCircle(1, 10 + &width, &height, &height);
}
```

It is important to remember that OPS83 is passing all values by reference, so if the drawing package expects actual values rather than pointers to values, you need to write a small piece of code to do that in the other language. For example, in C, `drawCircle()` might have been defined as follows:

```
void drawCircle(color, x, y, r)
int color, x, y, r;
{
  /* drawing code here */
}
```

If this is the case and we do not have the ability to modify the graphics package, then we must write a C function that first dereferences the variables.

```
void myDrawCircle(color, x, y, r)
int *color, *x, *y, *r;
{
   /* call the real draw_circle with the contents of the pointers */
   drawCircle(*color, *x, *y, *r);
}
```

9.11 SUMMARY

OPS5 is an excellent language for learning rule-based programming; however, it was not specifically designed for expert systems programming. Since many expert system problems tend to require both rule-based and imperative programming, some things tend to be very verbose in OPS5. OPS83 is a hybrid language that allows imperative programming and rule-based programming to be mixed. Calls to other languages such as C are easy. Large programs can be modularized as in other structured languages.

On the negative side, OPS83 has a more difficult syntax than OPS5, so it is not as easy to learn as a first programming language. In general, programming languages seem to become more difficult to learn as their power increases, and this is no exception.

OPS83 is a commercial product whose cost varies with the size of the machine. One must also have access to a C compiler, which means an additional expense on some machines. One big advantage over other expert system environments is that one can compile OPS83 programs and distribute the binaries without the full system. With OPS83, there is a modest charge for run-time licenses, but it is a fraction of the cost of delivering systems developed with other shells. Another important issue is the hardware requirement for developing and delivering the expert system. OPS83 is efficient enough to run well on a PC. Other shells can require powerful workstations with large memories and disks.

For more information on OPS83, contact Diana Connan, Vice President, Production Systems Technologies, 5001 Baum Boulevard, Pittsburgh, Pennsylvania, 15213, (412) 683-4000.

Another company offers tools for OPS83 programmers. The authors have not used these tools, but the manual is well written and contains a fair amount of detail. The toolkit is called *I.E. Tools for OPS83*, and it features a blackboard inspired control system, an exception processing system, and other utilities. For more information, contact Hybrid Technologies, 1119 Boynton Avenue, Bronx, New York, 10472, (212) 893-3048. This firm also offers OPS83 consulting and contract programming.

A

USING OPS5 on YOUR SYSTEM

A.1 INTRODUCTION

There are many OPS5 expert system environments available for almost every type of computer. The original OPS5 environment was developed at CMU and is in the public domain (free to the public). This environment can be run on a UNIX-based operating system and needs a LISP compiler. DEC and IBM also have their own versions of OPS5. We will not elaborate on these industrial versions of OPS5 because they all come with excellent documentation and support. DOS versions for the IBM PC environment are widely available and we have included a student version with this book to get you started.

A.2 USING PUBLIC DOMAIN OPS5 IN A NON-DOS (PC) ENVIRONMENT

If you want to use the public domain version, you should first find out if there is a specific version for your particular equipment (i.e., a SUN Microsystem version differs from a DEC-VAX version even though they may both be using UNIX). Also check to see if the LISP that you are using is compatible with the needs of the OPS5 that you are getting (e.g., there a versions that run on FRANZ LISP but will not run on COMMON LISP, and vice versa). Once you are satisfied that you are getting the right version of OPS5 and you have loaded it on your system, you must compile it in LISP. Once you have compiled it, then you can use the OPS5 environment by loading the program while in LISP. It is strongly suggested that you have a person with LISP experience around to help with the "minor" portability problems that may arise (e.g., we ran into a "case sensitivity" problem when we loaded OPS5 on our SUN's using COMMON LISP). When everything has been correctly loaded and compiled, then you can use OPS5. The following represents a sample session of using OPS5 on a SUN computer with COMMON LISP:

1. Log on to the system that you are using.
2. Invoke the LISP environment that is available.
3. Load the compiled version of OPS5 and the OPS5 package associated with it.
4. Now you can run load/run your OPS5 programs as described in the book.

Example of how to invoke the OPS5 environment on a SUN system:

```
Login

% Common Lisp
<loading your version of LISP>

cl>(load "ops5")
<loading your compiled version of OPS5>

cl>(in-package 'ops)
<introduces a new LISP environment to deal with OPS5>

** you are now in the OPS5 interpreter ****

cl>(load "lq.ops")
 .
 .
 .
cl>:exit
%
```

Note: You should use a function key or have your system operator create a single batch file to handle all of the above initialization of the system through a single command.

A.3 USING OPS5 IN A DOS (PC) ENVIRONMENT

There are several versions of OPS5 on the market and they all have their advantages and disadvantages. The aspects of a good software package that you should be concerned with are "ease of use," documentation, and operation, to name a few. Price is always a consideration, but a low price generally means that corners have been cut and you will pay later in time and frustration. Always investigate a product before you purchase (i.e., talk to people that have used the product; read reviews on the product; if possible, get an examination copy; etc.). We have included a student version of OPS5 that was designed especially for this book. We performed all the program development for this book on both versions and we were pleased with the ease of use, the documentation and support, and the enhanced features of the Sienna OPS5 environment. The disk has a "README" text file that explains how to load and run the environment which should get you up and programming in no time. We have included a short guide here to get you familiar with how to get Sienna OPS5 up and running:

1. You must have a PC with a DOS operating system.
2. Take the disk from the back of the book:
   - (a) If you only have a floppy disk system, make a backup copy of the disk and go to step 3.
   - (b) Load all the files from the floppy onto the hard disk (preferably in a separate directory).
3. The following files should be present on your hard disk or on the floppy in your main drive:

```
README.DOC     - This file
WORKBNCH.DOC   - Documentation on using the workbench
EDITOR.DOC     - Documentation on the editor
COMMANDS.DOC   - OPS5 commands available in the Student Version.
OPS5.EXE       - The Sienna OPS5 Workbench
EXARCH.OPS     - example program
EXAUTO.OPS     - example program
EXBAGIT.OPS    - example program
FILE.P         - data file
FILE.T         - data file
LQC1.OPS       - example program
```

4. To invoke the OPS5 environment:
   - (a) For floppy-only systems, enter the following:

     ```
     <drive letter>:OPS5
     ```
   - (b) For hard disk systems, enter the following when you are in the directory where OPS5 resides:

     ```
     OPS5
     ```
5. Now you will be in the Sienna OPS5 Workbench environment. To load a file, move the highlight in the top row to the INTERP column. Now hit the enter key and the OPS5 Interpreter will appear in the bottom window. To load files into the interpreter, use the "load" command. Example:

```
OPS5
> (load myprog.ops)
```

Notice that no quotes are used around the file MYPROG.OPS. If an MS-DOS pathname is used, any backslashed must be doubled. This is because a single backslash quotes the following character. Example:

```
OPS5
> (load d:\myprog.ops)
```

To leave the interpreter mode, hit the ESC key and this will put you back up in the workbench.

6. You can now run your programs as described in the book. All the files with the extension .DOC contain valuable information on how to use the Sienna-OPS5 environment, and these files should be read carefully and thoroughly.

B

DEBUGGING an OPS5 PROGRAM

The flow of an OPS5 program is sometimes confusing and difficult to follow. The reason is that the inference engine does not sequentially process the rules; the matching is effectively done in parallel. Also, the access tags play an important role in determining which of the rules are to be fired. There are two important things that the programmer will typically need to scrutinize in order to figure out how the program is running: the working memory (WM) and the conflict set (CS). OPS5 provides a debugging tool that will display the program's interaction with WM and CS. This tool is called *watch* and it has two or three levels, depending on the version of OPS5 that is being used. The level descriptions are:

- Watch 0. No trace
- Watch 1. Gives name of rules fired with time tags
- Watch 2. Gives name of rules fired with time tags and all interactions with WM
- Watch 3. Gives name of rules fired with time tags and all interactions with WM and shows all changes to the conflict set

You can find the level of watch that you are in by typing `(watch)` with no argument.

Other debugging tools provided by OPS5 are:

- Single Step. By using the `(run)` command with an argument, the programmer can put a limit on the maximum number of rules fired before returning to the command level, so for example, `(run 5)` would run the system until no rules could fire, up to a maximum of five cycles.

- Back Step. By using the `(back)` command with an argument for the number of cycles that the program is to back up by. For example, `(back 2)` would restore the state of working memory to what it was before the last two rules fired.
- Setting a Break Point. By using the `(pbreak)` command with an argument that is the name of the rule that you want to break (stop) the program at.

There are commands that show important information:

- WM. Displays the contents of WM, including access tags
- PM. Used with the name of a rule, will print out that rule
- CS. Displays the contents of the conflict set
- PPWM. Used with working memory patterns as arguments, will return all WM elements that match the argument
- MATCHES. Used with rule names as arguments, will return all WM elements that are matched to any LHS attributes in the rules

The following code is a copy of a simple debugging session with the LQ program. The purpose of this exercise is to help familiarize the reader with the essential concepts of debugging an OPS5 program. Note that I will use *italics* to enclose comments relevant to this appendix and not actually part of the debugging session.

*I am in the OPS5 shell and I will now load the OPS5 program. Notice that as the program is loaded, each rule is syntactically checked (an asterisk * signifies each rule that passes the check: there are four asterisks, which tells us that there are four rules in the program). Any syntax error will generate an error code related to the rule in which the error occurred. Syntax errors must be eliminated before the OPS5 program can be run. The LQ program in this example does not have any errors and the OPS5 shell prompt is displayed. Also note that the value "START" is loaded into WM as the LQ program is input into the OPS5 shell. This is signified by the symbol "=>WM:". The number "1" signifies the access tag for the class "START."*

```
OPS5 > (load lq.ops)
      * Loading file LQ.OPS ...
      =>WM:  1 : (START)
      * Production INSTANTIATE-WM compiled.
      * Production CHECK-SS-NUM compiled.
      * Production CHECK-DEBT-DISAPPROVE compiled.
      * Production CHECK-DEBT-APPROVE compiled.
OPS5 > (wm)
      1 : (START )
OPS5 > (watch)
      3
OPS5 > (run)
      end -- no productions true
```

The (wm) command above displays the contents of WM. We know this already because we saw it get loaded during the loading of LQ. The (watch) command above tells us what watch level we are in: 3. This is why the interaction with WM was displayed during the loading of LQ. Next we run the program by giving the command (run). Note that it ends with no firings. This is because the "start" class was stored in WM during the loading of the program. The OPS5 inference engine will not recognize this and therefore the program will not run (no rules fire). This a subtle point in OPS5 and will get you in trouble if you do not take care to understand it. I will now load "start" into WM from the interpreter and notice that as soon a the valid "start" is recognized, the conflict set receives the rule "instantiate-wm." Note that the number 2 that precedes the rule identifies the access tag(s) that are matched by the rule.

```
OPS5
 > (make start)
 =>WM:  2 : ( START )
 =>CS: INSTANTIATE-WM : 2
OPS5
 > (wm)
 1 : ( START )
 2 : ( START )
```

Now I can run the program. Notice that as values are removed from WM the arrow symbol is reversed: "<=". In this case the class is removed (see the "instantiate-wm" rule's first action). Also notice that there can be more than one rule in the CS and that the rules that are fired are identified by a firing sequence, name, and access tag matches. For example the rule "check-debt-disapprove" was the second rule to fire and matched with "applicant class Tom Tucker," which has the number 4 access tag in WM.

```
OPS5 > (run)
       1. INSTANTIATE-WM : 2
       <=WM:  2 : ( START )
       =>WM:  3 : ( APPLICANT ^NAME JOHN-SMITH ^SS-NUM 4742997 ^INCOME 60000
                  ^SAVINGS 50000 ^DEBT 15000 ^HALFINCOME-PLUS-SAVINGS 80000
                  ^DEBT-PLUS-HALFDEBT 22500 )
       =>CS: CHECK-DEBT-APPROVE : 3
       =>WM:  4 : ( APPLICANT ^NAME TOM-TUCKER ^SS-NUM NIL ^INCOME 40000
                  ^SAVINGS  25000  ^DEBT  100000  ^HALFINCOME-PLUS-SAVINGS
                  45000 ^DEBT-PLUS-HALFDEBT 150000 )
       =>CS: CHECK-DEBT-DISAPPROVE : 4
       =>CS: CHECK-SS-NUM : 4
       2. CHECK-DEBT-DISAPPROVE : 4
       =>WM:  5 : ( LOAN-ACTION ^DISAPPROVE TOM-TUCKER )
       3. CHECK-SS-NUM : 4
```

This is the displayed output from the "write" statements in the rule "check-ss-num."

```
Missing Social Security Number
Applicant's Name is  TOM-TUCKER
Enter Social Security Number  5555555
```

```
<=WM:  4 : ( APPLICANT ^NAME TOM-TUCKER ^SS-NUM NIL ^INCOME 40000
             ^SAVINGS 25000 ^DEBT 100000 ^HALFINCOME-PLUS-SAVINGS
              45000 ^DEBT-PLUS-HALFDEBT 150000 )
=>WM:  6 : ( APPLICANT ^NAME TOM-TUCKER ^SS-NUM 5555555 ^INCOME 40000
             ^SAVINGS  25000  ^DEBT  100000  ^HALFINCOME-PLUS-SAVINGS
             45000 ^DEBT-PLUS-HALFDEBT 150000 )
```

Notice that the class "Tom Tucker" is first removed from WM and then loaded back into WM with the new "SS-NUM" of 5555555. This is an idiosyncrasy of OPS5 that when a modify action is used, first the class is removed and then the class gets "made" (make command) again with the new date. All the old data remains the same but the access tag is updated.

```
        =>CS: CHECK-DEBT-DISAPPROVE : 6
        4. CHECK-DEBT-DISAPPROVE : 6
        =>WM:  7 : ( LOAN-ACTION ^DISAPPROVE TOM-TUCKER )
        5. CHECK-DEBT-APPROVE : 3
        =>WM:  8 : ( LOAN-ACTION ^DISAPPROVE NIL ^APPROVE JOHN-SMITH )
        end -- no productions true
OPS5 > (wm)
        1 : ( START )
        3 : ( APPLICANT ^NAME JOHN-SMITH ^SS-NUM 4742997 ^INCOME 60000
              ^SAVINGS 50000 ^DEBT 15000 ^HALFINCOME-PLUS-SAVINGS 80000
              ^DEBT-PLUS-HALFDEBT 22500 )
        5 : ( LOAN-ACTION ^DISAPPROVE TOM-TUCKER )
        6 : ( APPLICANT ^NAME TOM-TUCKER ^SS-NUM 5555555 ^INCOME 40000
              ^SAVINGS 25000 ^DEBT 100000 ^HALFINCOME-PLUS-SAVINGS 45000
              ^DEBT-PLUS-HALFDEBT 150000 )
        7 : ( LOAN-ACTION ^DISAPPROVE TOM-TUCKER )
        8 : ( LOAN-ACTION ^DISAPPROVE NIL ^APPROVE JOHN-SMITH )
OPS5 > (remove *)
        <=WM:  8 : ( LOAN-ACTION ^DISAPPROVE NIL ^APPROVE JOHN-SMITH )
        <=WM:  7 : ( LOAN-ACTION ^DISAPPROVE TOM-TUCKER )
        <=WM:  6 : ( APPLICANT ^NAME TOM-TUCKER ^SS-NUM 5555555 ^INCOME 40000
                     ^SAVINGS 25000 ^DEBT 100000 ^HALFINCOME-PLUS-SAVINGS 45000
                     ^DEBT-PLUS-HALFDEBT 150000 )
        <=WM:  5 : ( LOAN-ACTION ^DISAPPROVE TOM-TUCKER )
        <=WM:  3 : ( APPLICANT ^NAME JOHN-SMITH ^SS-NUM 4742997 ^INCOME 60000
                     ^SAVINGS 50000 ^DEBT 15000 ^HALFINCOME-PLUS-SAVINGS 80000
                     ^DEBT-PLUS-HALFDEBT 22500 )
        <=WM:  1 : ( START )
OPS5 > (wm)
        NIL
OPS5 >
```

The next section of debugging shows how you can set a break point at a rule. The program will stop when it is about to fire the rule and you can look at working memory, the conflict set, and so on. To start the program again, just type (run)

```
OPS5 > (make start)
       =>WM:  2 : ( START )
       =>CS: INSTANTIATE-WM : 2
```

I will set a break point at rule "CHECK-DEBT-APPROVE."

```
OPS5 > (pbreak CHECK-DEBT-APPROVE)
```

I will now check to make sure that the break point was set.

```
OPS5 > (pbreak)

       CHECK-DEBT-APPROVE

OPS5 > (RUN)
       6. INSTANTIATE-WM : 9
       <=WM:  9 : ( START )
       =>WM: 10 : ( APPLICANT ^NAME JOHN-SMITH ^SS-NUM 4742997 ^INCOME 60000
                  ^SAVINGS 50000 ^DEBT 15000 ^HALFINCOME-PLUS-SAVINGS 80000
                  ^DEBT-PLUS-HALFDEBT 22500 )
                =>CS: CHECK-DEBT-APPROV : 10
       =>WM: 11 : ( APPLICANT ^NAME TOM-TUCKER ^SS-NUM NIL ^INCOME 40000
                   ^SAVINGS 25000 ^DEBT 100000 ^HAKFINCOME-PLUS-SAVINGS 45000
                   ^DEBT-PLUS-HALFDEBT 150000 )
                =>CS: CHECK-DEBT-DISSAPPROV : 11
                =>CS: CHECK-SS-NUM : 11
                7. CHECK-DEBT-DISSAPPROV : 11
       =>WM: 12 : ( LOAN-ACTION ^DISSAPPROV TOM-TUCKER )
                8. CHECK-SS-NUM : 11


               Missing Social Security Number
               Applicant's Name is TOM-TUCKER
               Enter Social Security Number 66667

       <=WM: 11 : ( APPLICANT ^NAME TOM-TUCKER ^SS-NUM NIL ^INCOME 40000
                  ^SAVINGS 25000 ^DEBT 100000 ^HAKFINCOME-PLUS-SAVINGS 45000
                  ^DEBT-PLUS-HALFDEBT 150000 )
       =>WM: 13 : ( APPLICANT ^NAME TOM-TUCKER ^SS-NUM 66667 ^INCOME 40000
                  ^SAVINGS 25000 ^DEBT 100000 ^HALFINCOME-PLUS-SAVINGS 45000
                  ^DEBT-PLUS-HALFDEBT 150000 )
                =>CS: CHECK-DEBT-DISSAPPROV : 13
                9. CHECK-DEBT-DISSAPPROV : 13
                =>WM:  14 : ( LOAN-ACTION ^DISSAPPROV TOM-TUCKER )
                10. CHECK-DEBT-APPROV : 10
                =>WM:  15 : ( LOAN-ACTION ^DISSAPPROV NIL ^APPROV JOHN-SMITH)
               ***break***
```

At this point, OPS5 has given control back to the upper level and you can use any command to investigate the condition of the OPS5 environment at this point in the program. If you want to continue the operation, type (run) as shown below

```
OPS5
 > (RUN)
 end -- no productions true
OPS5
 > (WM)

 1 : ( START )
 3 : ( APPLICANT ^NAME JOHN-SMITH ^SS-NUM 4742997 ^INCOME 60000
     ^SAVINGS 50000 ^DEBT 15000 ^HALFINCOME-PLUS-SAVINGS 80000
     ^DEBT-PLUS-HALFDEBT 22500 )
 =>CS: CHECK-DEBT-APPROV : 10
 5 : ( LOAN-ACTION ^DISSAPPROV TOM-TUCKER )
 6 : ( APPLICANT ^NAME TOM-TUCKER ^SS-NUM 5555555 ^INCOME 40000
     ^SAVINGS 25000 ^DEBT 100000 ^HALFINCOME-PLUS-SAVINGS 45000
     ^DEBT-PLUS-HALFDEBT 150000 )
 7 : ( LOAN-ACTION ^DISSAPPROV TOM-TUCKER )
 8 : ( LOAN-ACTION ^DISSAPPROV NIL ^APPROV JOHN-SMITH )
10 : ( APPLICANT ^NAME JOHN-SMITH ^SS-NUM 4742997 ^INCOME 60000
     ^SAVINGS 50000 ^DEBT 15000 ^HALFINCOME-PLUS-SAVINGS 80000
     ^DEBT-PLUS-HALFDEBT 22500 )
12 : ( LOAN-ACTION ^DISSAPPROV TOM-TUCKER )
13 : ( APPLICANT ^NAME TOM-TUCKER ^SS-NUM 5555555 ^INCOME 40000
     ^SAVINGS 25000 ^DEBT 100000 ^HALFINCOME-PLUS-SAVINGS 45000
14 : ( LOAN-ACTION ^DISSAPPROV TOM-TUCKER )
15 : ( LOAN-ACTION ^DISSAPPROV NIL ^APPROV JOHN-SMITH )
OPS5
 >
```

End of debugging session.

This example should get you started with debugging an OPS5 program. The amount of time that you spend debugging can be reduced through careful program design and development. Always try to divide the problem into modules and then assign certain groups of rules to handle each module. Debugging can then be directed to individual modules first, with total integration of the modules only after they have been proven to work correctly.

Debugging has been called an art form and each individual must spend time to develop their own style. Don't be afraid to investigate and test new techniques. One last hint is to keep a bound notebook label "DEBUGGING NOTES" and continually critique your debugging sessions for future reference. Good Luck!

C

OPS5 SYNTAX

This is a description of OPS5 syntax from the OPS5 User's Manual, by Charles L. Forgy. It is in modified Backus-Naur Form. If you are not familiar with the notation, the symbols to the left of the ::= are called non-terminals. That means that they are composed of a series of non-terminals and terminals that appear to the right of the ::=. When there are multiple ::= symbols, either sequence on the right can be used. Things on the right in italics are non-terminals, and things in a normal typeface are terminals, which means that they literally appear in an OPS5 program.

Where a * appears on the right side, it means that the non-terminal preceding it can appear zero, one, or more times.

```
production          ::= ( p constant-symbolic-atom lhs --> rhs )

lhs                 ::=  positive-ce ce*

ce                  ::=  positive-ce
                    ::=  negative-ce

positive-ce         ::=  form
                    ::= { element-variable form }
                    ::= { form element-variable }

negative-ce         ::= - form

form                ::= ( lhs-term* )
```

```
lhs-term            ::= ^ constant-symbolic-atom lhs-value
                    ::= ^ number lhs-value
                    ::= lhs-value

lhs-value           ::= { restriction* }
                    ::= restriction

restriction         ::= << any-atom* >>
                    ::= predicate atomic-value
                    ::= atomic-value

atomic-value        ::= // any-atom
                    ::= var-or-const

var-or-const        ::= constant-symbolic-atom
                    ::= number
                    ::= variable

predicate           ::= =
                    ::= <>
                    ::= <
                    ::= <=
                    ::= >=
                    ::= >
                    ::= <=>

rhs                 ::= action*

action              ::= ( make rhs-term* )
                    ::= ( remove element-desig* )
                    ::= ( modify element-desig rhs-term* )
                    ::= ( halt )
                    ::= ( bind variable )
                    ::= ( bind variable rhs-term* )
                    ::= ( cbind element-variable )
                    ::= ( call constant-symbolic-atom rhs-term* )
                    ::= ( write rhs-term* )
                    ::= ( openfile rhs-term* )
                    ::= ( closefile rhs-term* )
                    ::= ( default rhs-term* )
                    ::= ( build quoted-form* )

element-desig       ::= number
                    ::= element-variable

rhs-term            ::= ^ var-or-constant rhs-value
                    ::= rhs-value
```

```
rhs-value               ::= atomic-value
                        ::= function

function                ::= ( litval var-or-const )
                        ::= ( substr element-des var-or-const var-or-const)
                        ::= ( genatom )
                        ::= ( crlf )
                        ::= ( rjust var-or-constant )
                        ::= ( tabto var-or-constant )
                        ::= ( accept )
                        ::= ( accept var-or-constant )
                        ::= ( acceptline var-or-constant* )
                        ::= ( compute expression )
                        ::= user-defined-function

user-defined-function   ::= ( constant-symbolic-atom var-or-const* )

expression              ::= number
                        ::= variable
                        ::= expression operator expression
                        ::= ( expression )

operator                ::= +
                        ::= -
                        ::= *
                        ::= //
                        ::= \\

quoted-form             ::= \\ rhs-value
                        ::= any-atom
                        ::= ( quoted-form* )
```

INDEX

A

accept, 32, 37, 57
acceptline, 32, 36, 57
access tags, 10, 11, 45
addition, 52
advantages of rule-based languages, 14
AND statement, 7
APL, 73
arithmetic operations, 52
arrays, 61, 68
attributes, 6
automobile diagnosis program, 115

B

backward chaining, 5, 15
base address, 62
bind, 33, 37, 62
binding variables, 27
bubble sort, 77
build, 33
building rules, 109
bulk data operations, 54

C

call, 33
casting, 164
cbind, 33
certainty factors, 114
chaining:
  backward, 5
  forward, 5
class, 6
classes, 19
closefile, 33
closing files, 55
computation, 29
compute, 30, 33, 52, 53, 59
conflict resolution, 10, 12, 15, 69
conflict resolution strategy, 47, 49, 51

conflict set, 10, 44, 48, 51
conjunction, 28
control, 4, 14, 40
control mechanism, 15
control strategy, 5
credit application, 83
crlf, 37
cycle, 11

D

data:
  large amounts of, 54
data files, 55
data structures, 163
debugging, 15
declaring working memory, 83
default, 33
delimiters, 56
DELTA, 4
demons, 51, 59
diagnosis:
  automobile, 115
discrimination net, 101
disjunction, 28
division, 52

E

element, 19
element class, 19
exit demons, 51
expertise, 14
extraction of knowledge, 5

F

factorials, 70
facts, 4, 6, 17
  stored, 7
files, 55
  closing, 55
  opening, 55
  reading, 55
firing rules, 8, 27
Forgy, Charles, 100, 162
forward chaining, 5, 15
functions, 169
  in OPS83, 164

G

genatom, 33
global variables, in OPS83, 164
grouping rules, 49

H

halt, 33
hierarchy, 71

I

IF-THEN structure, 7, 14, 22
imperative programming, 174
inf, 65
inference engine, 9, 10
infinite loops, 50
initialization of working memory, 19, 33, 41
interfacing with other languages, 119
interpreters, 163
iteration, 67, 69

K

knowledge extraction, 5
knowledge representation, 14, 15

L

large amounts of data, 54
left-hand side, 22, 26
LEX strategy, 44, 47
list, 61
literalize, 18
litval, 33, 62
load command, 26
loan qualification example, 26
local variables:
    in OPS83, 164
loops:
    infinite, 50

M

make, 19, 20, 21, 32, 33, 34, 41, 46
manipulating working memory, 42
matching, 26
mathematics, 52
means-ends analysis, 48
MEA strategy, 44, 48
memory, working, 17
modify, 21, 32, 34, 38, 46
modules, 49
modulo operator, 52
mortgage application, 82
multiplication, 52

N

negation, 70

O

one rule systems, 73
openfile, 33, 56, 57
opening files, 55
OPS2, 100
OPS83, 162

P

parameters:
    in OPS83, 164
partitioning rule sets, 71, 72, 85
Pascal, 67
pattern matching, 15, 73
pbreak, 35
procedures, 169
    in OPS83, 164
productions, 22
production system, 17
program flow, 42

R

R1, 3
reading files, 55
recency of time tags, 48
recursion, 67, 70
reducing complexity, 72
relational database, 73
remove, 20, 21, 32, 34, 42, 46
representation of knowledge, 14
reset, 57
resolution, conflict, 10
Rete algorithm, 30, 31
Rete network, 50
right hand side, 9, 20, 22
rule-based expert system, 14
rule based languages:
    disadvantages of, 15
rule firing, 27
rules, 4, 7, 10, 25
    building, 109
    firing, 8
    grouping, 49

S

side effects, 2
sorting, 77
sparse array, 70
start, 22
stored facts, 7, 10
strategy:
    conflict resolution, 47, 49, 51
structural similarity, 101
substr, 33, 64
subtraction, 52

T

tags:
    access, 45
    time, 45, 54
template, 18
temporal redundancy, 100
time tags, 10, 45, 46, 54
    recency of, 48
top level, 32
travelling salesman problem, 74
type coercion, 164
type declaration, in OPS83, 164

V

variable binding, 27
vector-attribute, 61
vectors, 61, 62

W

watch, 35
white space characters, 27
working memory, 6, 17
    initializing, 19, 33, 41
    manipulating, 42
write, 32, 36, 57

X

XCON, 3